A New King

A New King

Encountering the Risen Son

Paul S. Jeon

Foreword by
Brian Forman

WIPF & STOCK · Eugene, Oregon

A NEW KING
Encountering the Risen Son

Wipf & Stock
An Imprint of Wipf and Stock Publishers
199 W. 8th Ave., Suite 3
Eugene, OR 97401

www.wipfandstock.com

PAPERBACK ISBN: 978-1-5326-5017-8
HARDCOVER ISBN: 978-1-5326-5018-5
EBOOK ISBN: 978-1-5326-5019-2

Manufactured in the U.S.A.

In Honor of Cornelius Van Til,
William Edgar, and Scott Oliphint

Contents

Foreword

I CELEBRATED MY FIRST Easter nearly five years ago in 2013. It was a bitter-sweet experience. Traumatizing and liberating in the same moment. For the first time in my life, I began to process who Jesus was and is. Of all people—I was now a Christian? How could it be?

Not longer after, I met Paul Jeon. He regularly sought me out and met with me for coffee, dinner, dessert, errands, and so forth. Any excuse he could think of to meet with me, that's what he did. Once strangers, we soon became close friends and co-laborers for the gospel.

One day Pastor Paul told me about seminary (he had to explain what it was). It sounded like a great idea; I wanted to learn everything that I had missed out on for my entire life: the Bible, Christianity, the list goes on. So I went. From then onward, Paul wore many hats in my life: Dr. Jeon on campus, Pastor Paul in church, and Paul my friend the rest of the time. As I reflect on it now, Paul, like the apostle Paul before him, has been many things to many people (1 Corinthians 9:22), and for me he's been all things so that I might know Jesus Christ better through our relationship.

As someone who once hated Christianity (and especially Christians), I'm drawn to Paul because he loves conversing with all kinds of people—Christians, non-Christians, skeptics—you name it. I bring that up because whichever you are (and you are one of them), he wrote this book for you. There's no grand, lofty speech. Just raw honesty about the way things are for anyone who is human.

This book gets at an important question: "What is the Easter message?" If you think you know the answer, maybe you don't. That's not an insult, just a possible fact. Before I was a Christian, I thought I knew—and I didn't. The thing is, even if you think you know what Easter is, why not be sure of it?

Wherever you are in life, it makes me glad that you would pick up this book. In the same way I've benefited from Dr. Jeon's brilliant scholarship, Pastor Paul's guidance, and my friend Paul's humanness, I trust you will as well. Who knows, at the end of it all this might be the first Easter you celebrate.

Brian Forman
February 22, 2018

Acknowledgments

FIRST, I WANT TO thank my research assistant Brian Forman whose contributions are far too many to enumerate. Without his tireless and meticulous efforts, this book would have never come to fruition. Second, I thank the Burris family, the Oh family, and my siblings whose benefaction greatly facilitated the completion of this project. Third, I thank Tim Keller whose reflections on the last two chapters of Luke shaped both the structure and content of much of this book. He remains a model of humility and wisdom. Finally, I thank my family, especially my wife, and my church-family, NewCity, for making life and ministry such a delight.

Introduction

I HAVE BEEN A Christian for some years now. It's hard to know exactly how long. You could say that I "gave my life" to Jesus during a retreat at the age of ten. But I don't think I knew what the gospel meant at the time. All I knew was that Jesus had died for my sins and that if I believed in him, I would have eternal life. From that point, I began to read the Bible on a regular basis, was involved with my church's youth program, and suspected that at some point I would go to seminary.

It wasn't until my junior year at college that the gospel began to take on real substance. This happened through my college fellowship's study of Romans. It was during this time big words like justification and glorification began to make some sense. It was also during this time I was at a crossroad: should I continue on the path of finance or should I become a pastor? Not that one is inherently more spiritual than the other. By this point, I had accrued enough formal study and experience to have a working knowledge of what life as an investment banker would be like. But I still wasn't sure what it meant to be a pastor. I felt like what was critical to answering this question was getting to know Jesus much better. So I decided to take a break from finance and devoted the next several years to focused theological studies at Westminster Theological Seminary.

My formal theological education was rich. But even richer was the experience of encountering people who were very intelligent and who very much loved God. These people included professors and the student body, many of whom had already suffered much for the sake of making the gospel known. It was also during this period I encountered Jesus in a more personal and powerful way than ever before. It was probably some mix of focused theological study, actual pastoral experience, and extended times of reflection, quietness, and meditation that allowed for this. My conclusion from this time was that Jesus is a king like no other who *had* to be proclaimed—not because in some way he was an insecure being who required special attention, but because we live in a world desperately in need of the sort of hope he has brought by his resurrection.

I've enjoyed meeting many people over the years who take issue with Christianity. Many say they can't believe because the Christian faith doesn't square with any thinking and rational mind. But in my experience, most of such people have suffered some negative personal experience with Christianity. Some have been either abused by religious authority or know of others that have. Some have felt condemned. Others have engaged professing believers and have experienced nothing but "ungrace." All in all, they have said, "If that's Christianity, I want nothing to do with it."

It is most unfortunate that adherents of the faith continue to misrepresent the faith either by their teaching or their conduct (or both). But one thing I have become increasingly confident of is that a direct and personal encounter with the risen Son can change a person—perhaps even convert a person to believing that Jesus was the God-man who died for sinners and was raised for their glory. Gandhi purportedly said, "I like your Christ, I do not like your Christians." Perhaps a necessary first step, then, is to meet the Christ hidden behind the Christians. Who knows? By doing so—by encountering the Son—you may perhaps better understand and even come to love the terrible Christians for whom he died.

This book is purposefully short. It walks the reader through the last two chapters of Luke's Gospel—Jesus standing on trial

(1), Jesus dying on the cross (2), Jesus rising from the dead (3), Jesus walking with his disciples (4), and Jesus commissioning his disciples (5). Many commentators of the New Testament have noted how the last few chapters of each Gospel (Matthew, Mark, Luke, and John) represent Jesus at his essence—who he is and why he came. My hope is that this brief meditation on these final moments of his life on earth might elucidate what made Jesus so unique—why he is a king like no other. In the end, whether you come to believe in him as the risen Son, I trust that you will have a deep admiration of his life and ministry and perhaps even some reservation about keeping him at a safe distance. He desires to give us far more than anything we could ever ask or imagine. His invitation is to come and encounter him as the resurrected king.

1

The King on Trial

Luke 23:1–25

WE BEGIN OUR REFLECTIONS on the last two chapters of Luke's Gospel with Jesus standing on trial before Pilate for crimes of treason. Pilate is puzzled about Jesus, but in a sense this comes as no surprise. In each Gospel (Matthew, Mark, Luke, John) it is clear that Jesus defies simplistic categories. He is, after all, the Lion and the Lamb. But Pilate is especially confused because the man standing before him lacks any regal presence. Despite all the buzz surrounding him, he seems at best ordinary. Through such irony, Luke invites his readers to reconsider the basic question of greatness: what does it mean to be a king in God's kingdom? What is true greatness?

Is Jesus a King?

Pilate is confused. Who is this pitiful man standing before him, face bruised and hands tied? Why are the Jewish leaders accusing him of one crime after another? He doesn't look like a criminal. Why are they bringing this Jesus of Nazareth to the Roman governor in Jerusalem?

The accusers cry out, "We found this man misleading our nation and forbidding us to give tribute to Caesar, and saying that he himself is Christ, a king" (Luke 23:2). The final phrase catches Pilate's attention. This man claims to be a king? This is unsettling.[1] Pilate's job is to ensure that no one sets himself up against Caesar.

Pilate looks at the prisoner and asks, "Are you the King of the Jews?" (23:3). Pilate is not a religious Jew who has diligently studied the Hebrew Scriptures. His question does not mean "Are you the One promised in the Law and the Prophets?" Pilate only wants to know whether Jesus poses a threat to Rome. Jesus doesn't look like king. Instead, he looks like a "pitiful specimen . . . one of Rome's deranged who claimed to be Caesar."[2]

Pilate concludes that Jesus is harmless. But his accusers persist, and it comes out that Jesus is from Galilee. So Pilate sees an out. Galilee is under the jurisdiction of the tetrarch Herod Antipas, who just happens to be in Jerusalem. Pilate decides to pack Jesus off to stand trial before Herod. Let him be Herod's problem. If anyone had the knack to silence Jesus's threat to Rome, it was Herod. The concern for power and how to hold on to it was instilled in him from a young age by his father Herod the Great. In the Herod family, if you were a threat to power, you were killed.[3]

Herod is no stranger to Jesus. He has heard about Jesus and is "perplexed" by him (9:7–9; 23:8). He's heard of Jesus's ability to heal people of demons and disease (8:26–48). There

---

1. Scholar Jack Dean Kingsbury observes: "Upon hearing Jesus accused of being Messiah, a king, Pilate concentrates his inquiry on this" (*Conflict in Luke*, 65).

2. Yancey, *Jesus I Never Knew*, 198–99. Similarly, Bruce, *Jesus*, 104: "Jesus, to [Pilate's] way of thinking, was a harmless lunatic, not the stuff of which rebels were made."

3. For further details, see Yamazaki-Ransom, *Roman Empire in Luke's Narrative*, 163–72; Dicken, *Herod as a Composite Character in Luke-Acts*, 45–70; Bruce, *New Testament History*, 20–31.

are even rumors that he can resurrect the dead (8:49–56). Now, to Herod's surprise and delight, this miracle-worker is standing before him thanks to Pilate. He longs to see what kind of power Jesus really has.

To his great disappointment Jesus refuses to put on a show. He doesn't do anything.[4] Herod begins to think that Jesus isn't so powerful after all. But perhaps he is eloquent in speech. Indeed, if Jesus can gather crowds to himself, he is a force to be reckoned with. And so, Herod wants to hear him speak: ". . . he questioned him at some length, but he made no answer" (23:9). Herod concludes that the reports must have been exaggerated. Before him stands nothing but a weak and pathetic man who has wasted his time. In response, "Herod with his soldiers treated him with contempt and mocked him. Then, arraying him in splendid clothing, he sent him back to Pilate" (23:11).

Both Pilate and Herod arrive at the same conclusion—Jesus is innocent. Luke highlights this several times:

"I find no guilt in this man" (23:4).

". . . I did not find this man guilty of any of your charges against him. Neither did Herod, for he sent him back to us. Look, nothing deserving death has been done by him" (23:14–15).

"I have found in him no guilt deserving death" (23:22).

Now, to be clear, when Pilate and Herod declare Jesus innocent, it is not because they are concerned with justice. This is clear from the way Herod mocks Jesus and the way Pilate later surrenders to the crowd. Their only concern is whether Jesus is

---

4. Kingsbury observes the reasoning: ". . . Jesus does not perform miracles on demand, for their purpose is to summon to repentance (10:13). Because Antipas [Herod] is spiritually 'blind' to the need for repentance, the reader knows not to anticipate that Jesus will satisfy his wish" (*Conflict in Luke*, 65). Similarly, Jensen, *Herod Antipas in Galilee*, 119: "Antipas is clearly depicted as an opponent of Jesus whose evil deeds render him unworthy of hearing or seeing, and who plays a role in the fulfillment of the prophecy of Isaiah 53."

an aspiring king looking to set himself up against Caesar. Their conclusion: obviously not.

But perhaps their conclusion was premature. In his response to Pilate's question "Are you the King of the Jews?" (23:3), Jesus never flat-out denies being a king. His answer is deliberately vague: "You have said so" (23:3). The Greek literally reads, "You say." His response has a positive connotation, but it neither affirms nor denies his kingship. Jesus doesn't say, "Yes, I am," nor does he say, "No, I'm not."

Suppose you and I go out for a meal. We eat, and then the bill comes but it has already been paid. I ask, "Did you pay the bill?" You reply, "You say so." Confused, I ask again: "Wait, did you pay the bill or not?" Again you reply, "You say so." Now, more confused and a bit flustered, I ask one last time: "So, is that a *yes* or a *no*—seriously, what are you saying?"

When Jesus replies to Pilate, he is being intentionally ambiguous. He is saying: "Yes, I am a king, but not the kind of king you're thinking of. I'm a king like the world has never seen."[5] Pastor Robert J. Dean explains: "Jesus wasn't playing the same game as Pilate . . . Jesus is the king of the Jews, but not in a way that a power-broker like Pilate could ever understand."[6]

Like the Roman rulers, the Jewish chief priests and scribes misunderstand Jesus's kingship. They suppose that Jesus cares about the things they care about—worldly influence, authority, and esteem. Consequently, they feel threatened by his growing popularity and seek to destroy him. They do so by morphing his claim to be "the Son of God" (22:70) into a political challenge of insurrection.[7] This was necessary because

---

5. Skinner agrees, observing that Jesus's response "suggests that he and Pilate have different understandings of kingship" (*Trial Narratives*, 78).

6. Dean, *Leaps of Faith*, 119.

7. Immediately before Jesus's trial with Pilate was his trial with the Jewish leaders (Luke 22:66–71). There the main accusation was Jesus's claim to be "the Son of God" (i.e., equal with God), which was something the Jews considered blasphemy and deserving of death. However, with Pilate the accusation clearly

Jews could not legally put anyone to death. Bible scholar F. F. Bruce explains:

> Pilate would not be interested in the charge of blasphemy . . . but he could not overlook the charge of sedition. Since Jesus had virtually claimed to be king of the Jews, Pilate (it was hoped) would simply rubber-stamp the decision of the high priest and his colleagues that Jesus had committed a capital offense, and order the death sentence to be carried out.[8]

Unlike Pilate and Herod, the Jewish leaders conclude that Jesus is guilty and deserving of death for blasphemy. But not unlike Pilate and Herod, they see Jesus in worldly terms: he is a threat to their rule.

Finally, like the Roman rulers and Jewish leaders, even Jesus's disciples view him from the same lenses of worldly power. Initially they follow him because they believe he will establish a new earthly kingdom. The two disciples on the road to Emmaus say of Jesus: he "was a prophet mighty in deed and word before God and all the people . . . we had hoped that he was the one to redeem Israel" (24:19–21). Repeatedly, all the disciples argue about who will be the greatest in his kingdom (9:46; 22:24). Unlike the Roman rulers and Jewish leaders, the disciples lack status and influence. And on the surface it appears they are devoted to Jesus. But a closer examination reveals that the only true difference is that one group has power, the other does not. Both, however, understand—and lust for—the same kind of power.

This attitude toward power is pervasive today, not just in the "secular" world but also in the "sacred." In pastoral ministry, greatness is often defined according to worldly standards. What

---

and intentionally shifts. Yancey observes: "On the way to the Roman judges, the implications of the *Messiah* [i.e., *Christ*] claim changed from blasphemy to sedition. The word [*Christ*] did mean king, after all, and Rome had no tolerance for any agitator who professed such a title" (*Jesus I Never Knew*, 198).

8. Bruce, *Jesus*, 102.

is success in ministry? Success is becoming a celebrity pastor, leading a megachurch, and writing a bestseller.[9] Being an "ordinary pastor" is no longer acceptable.[10]

Jesus Redefines Greatness

Jesus's ambiguous response was not just for Pilate. It is for everyone. He did not deny his kingship, but he knew that no one would understand the sort of king he is unless he uprooted traditional understandings of power and greatness.

In his life and ministry this uprooting was realized. He did not make it his life's ambition to acquire power. He did not use signs and wonders to elevate his status. He did not use his speech to manipulate the crowds. Instead, he gave up his status, riches, and comforts to become a servant and die on the cross to save and exalt others. Pastor Tim Keller comments: "Because Jesus was the king who became a servant, we see a reversal of values in his kingdom administration (Luke 6:20–26). . . Though he was the greatest, he made himself the servant of all. . . This is a complete reversal of the world's way of thinking . . ."[11]

Jesus showed that the way up is down. Most people want to get richer; Jesus became poor. Most want more status; Jesus surrendered his glory. Most seek power and security; Jesus made himself vulnerable and weak. As the ambiguous "King of the Jews" (23:3), Jesus redefined what it means to be a king in the kingdom of God.

---

9. Professor of Church History Carl R. Trueman blogs on the topic of celebrity pastors, saying: "The American church reflects the culture: ministries built around individuals, around big shots, churches that focus on god-like guru figures, all of them pointing to one door" ("Messiahs Pointing at the Door").

10. For an excellent counter-narrative to that of celebrity ministry, see Carson, *Memoirs of an Ordinary Pastor*.

11. Keller, *Center Church*, 46–47.

Indeed, Jesus's reversal of the world's perspective on greatness is so radical that it is easy to see why no one understood the sort of king he came to be. "Racial and class superiority, accrual of money and power at the expense of others, yearning for popularity and recognition—all are marks of living in the world. They represent the opposite of the gospel mind-set."[12] Jesus displayed none of these marks. Instead, he came to show that he is a king who suffers *with* his people and a king who suffers *for* his people. In doing so, he invites everyone in every generation to take a step back and reconsider the meaning of greatness.

The King Who Suffers with His People

Suffering and injustice are inescapable. Take the example of Hawra', an innocent girl caught in the ravages of war:

> "I want my mommy," Hawra' mumbles . . . Her face is etched with small wounds, gauze wrapped around her throat and leg over burns that have yet to heal. She can't open her eyes; there is shrapnel in one of them, the other painfully closed. Doctors don't know if she will be able to see properly again. . . . She keeps asking for her mother who died in the airstrikes.[13]

Hawra's grandmother says: "I am thinking it's better to be dead. I am thinking to die, rather than a life like this. [Hawra'] was like a little flower. She would play and run. Now, she has no mother, no eyes."[14]

It is hard to make sense of such injustice. The Bible says that there is a God who is all-powerful and good. But if this is the case, why does he allow suffering to persist? Many people who are seeking answers to why there is evil in the world find

12. Ibid., 47.

13. Damon, Balkiz, and Laine, "Why ISIS Offered to Kill this 4-Year-Old Girl."

14. Ibid.

it hard to believe in the God of the Bible. Renowned sociologist Peter Berger aptly relates how the problem of evil and any explanation for it finds its pinnacle confrontation with the God of the Bible:

> [I]f not only all power but all ethical values are ascribed to the one God who created all things in this or any other world, then the problem of theodicy becomes a pointed question directed to this very conception. Indeed, more than in any other religious constellation, it may be said that this type of monotheism stands or falls with its capacity to solve the question of theodicy. . .[15]

The fact of evil and injustice in the world is a real and understandable struggle for any Christian—indeed, as much as for any atheist. Keller notes that disbelieving in God "doesn't make it any easier."[16] Apologist William Edgar explains:

> [T]he problem of evil is not specifically a Christian problem. Those who struggle with evil have recognized that something is good and right, and yet things have gone wrong. Anyone who has a "problem" of evil admits to a standard, and thus to the need to reconcile the reality and the standard.[17]

The problem of evil and injustice cannot be answered by logic alone. If you have ever engaged a person that is angry with God, you know that there is as much emotion as there

---

15. Berger, *Sacred Canopy*, 73. The term "theodicy" refers to the problem of evil.

16. Keller, "With All This Suffering."

17. Edgar, *Reasons of the Heart*, 96. Responding to the late atheist Christopher Hitchens, Douglas Wilson articulates how atheism isn't actually the solution to "the problem of evil" that it presents itself to be; rather a deeper problem emerges in atheism that cannot be resolved: "With regard to . . . 'God's coexistence with evil,' I reply that I would rather have my God *and* the problem of evil than your no God and 'Evil? No problem!'" (*Is Christianity Good for the World?* 55).

is reason involved.[18] Christian apologist Ravi Zacharias observes: "But in demanding an answer for the reality of suffering, the questioner is looking for an emotionally satisfying answer as much or perhaps even more than for an intellectually fulfilling answer."[19]

Luke provides an "emotionally satisfying" and "intellectually fulfilling" answer in Christ. In the trial scenes, Jesus suffers in three ways: the legal system fails him, the Jewish leaders slander him, and the crowds turn on him.

First, Jesus is denied justice. Pilate and Herod repeatedly declare that Jesus is innocent. They cannot find any reason to punish him. "It is a stunning development that even Herod, who previously expressed his intention to kill Jesus [Luke 13:31], cannot find a reason to justify executing him now that he has him in custody."[20] Yet, in the end Jesus is condemned. If ever the "system" failed a person, it failed Jesus.[21] Scholar Pyung Soo Seo points out: "*In spite of* his threefold declaration of Jesus' innocence, Pilate gave a wrong verdict. . . Through Jesus' trial, Luke shows that the Roman judicial system, despite its emphasis on justice, could not protect the innocent, such as Jesus."[22]

Second, as noted already, the Jewish leaders misrepresent Jesus.[23] There is no basis for any of their charges. Jesus never

18. This is seen, for example, in Loftus's *Why I Became an Atheist*, 26, 30, 32, 34.

19. Zacharias, "Question," 9.

20. Skinner, *Trial Narratives*, 80.

21. The point is timeless and could be said of our justice system today, as Jarvis and Johnson suggest: "Jesus' fate exposes the lack of integrity, the impotence, and the true depths of oppression found in worldly political powers" (eds., *Feasting on the Gospels*, 317). For a powerful account of contemporary systemic injustice, see Stevenson's *Just Mercy*.

22. Seo, *Luke's Jesus in the Roman Empire*, 51. Similarly, Lee, "Pilate and the Crucifixion," 103: "[Pilate] essentially says, 'Jesus is innocent, therefore go ahead and execute him.'"

23. Scholar F. F. Bruce rightly notes how the Gospels present both the Gentiles and Jews as responsible: "There has been a tendency in recent times to

encouraged the crowds to rebel (23:5), nor did he forbid them from paying taxes (23:2). In fact, Jesus had told them to "render to Caesar the things that are Caesar's" (20:25). At best, the only accusation with some validity was Jesus's claim to be a king (23:2). But even this, as we have also noted already, was not entirely true. He was not the sort of king that Rome would have identified as a political threat.

Third, the crowds betray Jesus, shouting, "Crucify, crucify him!" (23:21). New Testament professor Robert C. Tannehill points out, "Three times they shout for Jesus' death . . . making clear that the people, not just the leaders, are participating."[24] This is disturbing because throughout Luke's Gospel the crowds benefited the most from Jesus's ministry. He taught them, healed them, and fed them (e.g., 5:15; 9:11–17). Imagine what it must have felt like to have the people you love suddenly turn on you? Only a few days earlier this same crowd had welcomed Jesus into Jerusalem, declaring, "Blessed is the King who comes in the name of the Lord!" (19:38).

In sum, Jesus was no stranger to injustice and suffering.

Christ's participation in human suffering is a unique feature of the Christian faith. "Only in Christ do we have a God who loves us enough to suffer with us."[25] Jesus did not stay at a safe distance but joined in our suffering. Though in very nature God, he made himself nothing, taking on human form and

---

ascribe the initiative in the final action against Jesus exclusively to the Roman authorities in Judaea. This has been in part a reaction against the monstrous calumny which has branded the whole Jewish nation of that day, and indeed of succeeding days, with responsibility for Jesus' death. . . It must indeed be emphasized that Jesus was sentenced to death by a Roman judge and executed by Roman soldiers. . . On the other hand, the testimony of the New Testament writers ascribes the initiative to the temple authorities, and this is confirmed by the earliest Jewish references to the trial and execution of Jesus. This cannot be explained entirely in terms of a desire to exonerate the Roman administration from responsibility in the matter" (Jesus, 96–97).

24. Tannehill, Narrative Unity of Luke-Acts, 164.

25. Vitale, "Response at the Cross," 84.

becoming obedient to death, even death on a cross (Philippians 2:6–8). Apologist Scott Oliphint comments:

> In all of God's dealings with creation, even as he takes to himself created properties, there is . . . a graciously free and willing humiliation that, when understood properly, should serve only to humble and amaze the hearts of any who have seen this voluntary condescension for what it truly is.[26]

No other religion can make this sort of claim.

We know from experience that a deep connection forms when you meet a person that can empathize with your pain. I was reminded of this recently when I arranged a dinner between two families. Both had struggled with infertility for many years. By grace one was finally able to conceive through special treatment. The other had already suffered several miscarriages and was pondering different options. As the two couples sat down as strangers, immediately a bond formed when they spoke of all the confusion, pain, hurt, and even laughter they had both experienced. At one point, one lady shared, "What I've wanted more than anything else over the years is someone who can not just sympathize but also empathize. Thank you for taking time to meet with me, to assure me that I'm not alone."[27]

William L. White explains the importance and power of such connections:

---

26. Oliphint, *God With Us*, 222.

27. Similarly, pastor A. J. Swoboda relates: "Each month, we'd drive down to the infertility clinic with our tail between our reproductive legs hoping this would be the month it finally happened. We made friends at the infertility clinic. It's shocking how easy it is to start a conversation with someone in the waiting room at an infertility clinic. You'd think it would be awkward. Nope. You go to the DMV or the doctor's office and people won't even look at each other. But there, in that little infertility waiting room, strangers were immediate friends. I think it's because that was one place in the whole world where infertile people could be understood for what they were going through. There, and only there, somebody else got what it was like" (*Glorious Dark*, 85).

When we speak of "recovery community," these qualities take on added significance because of the shared wounds its members bring to their membership in this community... It is here that, in discovering one's self in the stories of others, people discover themselves and a "narrative community" whose members not only exchange their stories but possess a "shared story."[28]

In Jesus we encounter someone that possesses our "shared story" of suffering. He knows what it is like to endure injustice, slander, and betrayal.

Does this reality fully resolve the problem of evil? No. But it helps. Quite a bit in fact. Edgar puts it well:

... a God who would go to the extent he did in the sufferings and victory of Christ is a God who will work all things out in the very best way. This may not explain everything about the outrage of evil, such as Auschwitz, AIDS, or the death of a child, but [this] overcomes it.[29]

We will not know in full why God allows suffering. But in Jesus we know that we will never suffer alone. He is a king who suffers with his people.

The King Who Suffers for His People

Not only does Jesus suffers *with* us; he also suffers *for* us.

Matthew's Gospel fills in some details of Jesus's trial: "Now at the feast the governor was accustomed to release for the crowd any one prisoner whom they wanted" (Matthew 27:15). Pilate decides to bring forth the notorious prisoner Barabbas, "a man who had been thrown into prison for an insurrection started in the city and for murder" (Luke 23:19). He reasons: "I want to release Jesus but the crowds want to crucify him. I'll put forward a real criminal! Surely the crowd will ask to release Jesus."

28. White, *Recovery Monographs*, 162–63.
29. Edgar, *Reasons of the Heart*, 105.

In Aramaic "Barabbas" means "son of the father."[30] Thus what you have in this scene is a "son of the father" standing next to *the* Son of the Father. Barabbas is clearly guilty; Jesus is clearly innocent. Pastor John Kimbell comments: "Luke stresses the guilt of Barabbas (23:19, 25) and puts him in direct contrast with the innocent Jesus (esp. v. 25). At the very least, there is remarkable irony that Jesus had been charged in essence with one of the very crimes for which Barabbas has been condemned."[31]

It appears that Pilate has found a way out of his dilemma. But the Jewish leaders and the crowds crush his hope, crying out, "Away with this man, and release to us Barabbas" (23:18). Luke indicates that "Pilate addressed them once more, desiring to release Jesus, but they kept shouting, 'Crucify, crucify him!'" (23:20–21). The situation is so unbelievable that Pilate pleads with them a third time (23:22). However, in the end "Pilate decided that their demand should be granted" (23:24). No one knows better than Pilate that the innocent is condemned, the guilty are free. No one except for perhaps Barabbas.

Barabbas knows he is a guilty man. He had started a rebellion and even killed a person. According to Roman law he should be put to death. Behind bars, when he hears the crowd shouting, "Crucify, crucify him!" (23:21), he assumes the hour has come. The Roman soldiers walk in, drag him outside, place him in front of the shouting crowd, and then . . . they release him. Confused, he turns to the soldiers and asks, "What's going on?" One of the soldiers points to Jesus and says, "That man is dying in your place."

30. Although the New Testament was recorded in Greek, Aramaic was one of the languages spoken in Jerusalem at the time. *Bar* means "son," and *abba* means "father."

31. Kimbell, *Atonement in Lukan Theology*, 71. New Testament professor John T. Carroll similarly observes that "the scene's irony is biting. The prefect frees a murderer—the name Barabbas receding behind his alleged crimes as his identity—and delivers the righteous man Jesus to the fate demanded by his adversaries among his own people" (*Luke*, 460). Perhaps, as Bruce adds, "the irony of the situation . . . was probably not lost on Pilate himself" (*Jesus*, 104).

No one knows for sure, but perhaps Barabbas made his way to Calvary to see Jesus hanging on the cross. Like none else in history, Barabbas could literally say "In my place condemned he stood."[32] Though guilty, Barabbas is now free. Though innocent, Jesus is condemned. This is the essence of the gospel: Jesus died for sinners. New Testament scholar N. T. Wright notes:

> It is one thing for Jesus to go in to eat with a man who is a sinner. It is a considerable step beyond that for him to go off and die the death of a violent rebel. But this is in fact the climax and focus of the whole *gospel*. This is the point for which Luke has been preparing us all along. All sinners, all rebels, all the human race are invited to see themselves in the figure of Barabbas; and, as we do so, we discover in this story that Jesus comes to take our place, under condemnation for sins and wickedness great and small. In the strange justice of God, which overrules the unjust "justice" of Rome and every human system, God's mercy reaches out where human mercy could not, not only sharing, but in this case substituting for, the sinner's fate.[33]

Jesus is the king who suffers *with* us and he is the king who suffers *for* us. Is he a king? Luke asserts he is indeed a king—but like none that has come before and after.

True Greatness

In his trial and suffering, Jesus redefines greatness. The normal pattern in history is for kings to do everything possible to preserve their power. But Jesus is completely different: he surrenders his status, suffers with his people, and ultimately dies in their place.

32. Bliss, "Hallelujah! What a Savior!" pub. 1875. Public domain.
33. Wright, *Luke for Everyone*, 279–80.

King David is considered the greatest king in Israel's history. But what did he do with his power? He committed adultery with Bathsheba, the wife of his loyal soldier Uriah. And how did he "atone" for sin? He sent Uriah to die on the frontline of battle so that by the servant's death the king would live. By contrast, what do we see in Jesus? He himself went to the frontline so that by the king's death the servants are free. Jesus's kingship presents a complete uprooting of worldly structures and givens in life.

What is greatness in the kingdom of God? It is Christ the king.

2

The King Dies

Luke 23:26–49

THE TRIAL SCENES CONCLUDE with Jesus's condemnation. As the narrative progresses, we expect Luke to go into details about Jesus's crucifixion. But he does not. Instead, he draws our attention to some of the people present at the cross and outlines their progression from ignorance to insight.

Universal Ignorance

In his last moments of life, Jesus does not hurl insults at his opponents. He does not express sorrow for himself. He does not display any outrage over the situation. No. He simply prays for his enemies: "Father, forgive them, for they *know not* what they do" (23:34). His prayer provides the best assessment of the situation: no one understands who he is and why he must suffer and die.

Luke begins this portrait of universal ignorance by focusing on the women who accompany Jesus to his death. This is unexpected because in his Gospel Luke always portrays women in a positive way. Even now, though Jesus's disciples have abandoned him, the women remain at his side.[1]

Imagine the walk to Calvary from their perspective. Jesus is so weak from hours of torture that he is unable to carry his cross (23:26).[2] As the women look at his pitiful estate, they think: "Why is this happening to him? This is a tragedy!" But hearing the women "mourning and lamenting for him" (23:27), Jesus turns and says: "Daughters of Jerusalem, do not weep for me, but weep for yourselves and for your children. For behold, the days [of judgment] are coming . . ." (23:28–29). From their perspective, Jesus's situation appears terrible; from his perspective, their situation is far worse. Kingsbury comments, "The point of the proverb, 'For if they do this when the wood is green, what will happen when it is dry?' (23:31), seems to be: What is about to befall me cannot be compared with what will befall the inhabitants of Jerusalem."[3]

In his response to the women Jesus is quoting Hosea 10:8, which in context describes an imminent event—the coming destruction of Jerusalem about forty years later in A.D. 70. However, Revelation 6:16, which also references this Old Testament text, indicates that this historical disaster foreshadows

---

1. Rather than professional mourners, these "women who were mourning and lamenting for him" (23:27) were comprised the "women who had come with him from Galilee" (23:55), namely "Mary Magdalene and Joanna and Mary the mother of James and the other women with them" (24:10). See Edwards, *The Gospel according to Luke*, 699.

2. Jesus had been beaten by the Jewish leaders (22:63), then beaten and scourged by the Roman guards (Mark 15:15, 19). The scourging, via a whip with pieces of metal and bone attached at the end, would have all but destroyed his body. The visible condition of Jesus and his body would have been a traumatic sight for anyone to see, especially for the women who cared about him.

3. Kingsbury, *Conflict in Luke*, 67. Similarly, Forbes and Harrower observe: "The fact that Jesus turned to give his attention to the women despite his excoriation and death sentence reveals a strong deliberateness about this action. The mere fact that he says something to the women is thus as significant as it is surprising. Jesus took the attention off his own immediate predicament and focused on their plight" (*Raised from Obscurity*, 126).

a greater judgment—God's eternal condemnation of sinners.[4] Thus, when Jesus says to the women "do not weep for me, but weep for yourselves and for your children" (23:28), he is calling them to repent lest they suffer final and eternal judgment. Jesus wants these kind and faithful women to understand that God's coming wrath against sin is far worse than the torture Jesus is enduring. New Testament scholar Darrell Bock observes:

> Jesus responds to their sense of remorse by redirecting their attention to a more serious issue. He urges them not to weep for him. . . The real issue moves beyond what Jesus will suffer to what his death means for those who reject him. . . How painful it is to be the object of God's wrath.[5]

Luke continues the theme of universal ignorance by shifting to Jesus's encounters with the Jewish leaders, the Roman soldiers, and the first criminal. All three interact with Jesus in basically the same way. As the iron nails impale and press Jesus's hands and feet to the cross, the Jewish leaders ridicule him: "He saved others; let him save himself, if he is the Christ of God, his Chosen One!" (23:35). The soldiers also mock him: "If you are the King of the Jews, save yourself!" (23:37). Finally, one of the criminals joins the verbal assault: "Are you not the Christ? Save yourself and us!" (23:39). Ignorance surrounds Jesus: no one understands why Jesus does not save himself.

Theologian John Calvin penned the words: "Nearly all the wisdom we possess, that is to say, true and sound wisdom, consists of two parts: the knowledge of God and of ourselves."[6] Here, the Jewish leaders, Roman soldiers, and criminal lack a

---

4. Professor Michael B. Shepherd's statement captures the overarching implications: "Jesus—and thus Luke—clearly understands Hos 10:8b in an eschatological sense (cf. Rev 6:16). The coming tribulation, not something from the past, will be greater than that of the present, so much so that the people will prefer death to life" (*Twelve Prophets*, 16).

5. Bock, *Luke: The NIV Application Commentary*, 594.

6. Calvin, *Institutes*, 1.1.1, 35.

proper knowledge of themselves and thus cannot have a proper knowledge of Christ. Because they do not see themselves as guilty people and therefore objects of divine wrath, they mock Jesus. They do not realize that in order to save them, Jesus cannot save himself. Author John Gillman observes: "Unwittingly their taunt for Jesus to save himself gets right to the heart of the gospel paradox. For if Jesus does yield to the temptation to save himself by holding on to his life . . . he will not be able to accomplish God's plan of redeeming those he was sent to save."[7]

Now, while the Jewish rulers and Roman soldiers challenge Jesus to "save himself," the criminal adds, "Save yourself *and* us!" (23:39). This is striking. Of all people, how could this criminal make such a demand on Jesus? It almost appears as if the criminal is making a deal with Jesus: "Right now I'm in a bad situation. But if you get me out of this, I'll believe in you."

Phrased in this way, the criminal's demand seems less foreign. In fact, it sounds very familiar. Many have made similar bargains: "God, if you're really there, if you really exist, get me out of this situation! And if you do, I'll live for you." In the movie *The Grey*, the protagonist John Ottway (played by Liam Neeson) faces a pack of vicious wolves. Near the end of the movie, he's alone, desperate, and despondent. At his wits' end he looks upward and whimpers: "Do something. Do something." Nothing happens. In despair, Ottway shrinks back into the snow and says, "I'll do it myself."[8] Like the first criminal (and many of us today), Ottway wants a relationship with God that is driven by "an entitled sense of ownership over God's sovereignty."[9]

7. Gillman, *Luke*, 199–200. The situation is not very different today. Dick Keyes observes (*Seeing through Cynicism*, 114): "The death of Christ confused people at the time it happened, just as it still confuses people today. Most people did not and still do not realize that something so radical was needed for their own salvation—simply that they would need that much saving. The cross has never made sense to those who see themselves as decent, respectable, confident people who simply want to add a spiritual dimension to their lives. They are apt to feel insulted by its implications."

8. Screenplay for *The Grey* by Joe Carnahan and Ian Mackenzie Jeffers.

9. Swoboda, *Dusty Ones*, 130.

Viewed this way, God's lordship is conditioned not on his being Creator but on his willingness to meet our demands.

While the request "if you do this, I will believe in you" is understandable, there is an assumption in it, namely that we know better than God how our lives should play out. However, isn't it possible that God has purposes that are good but hidden from us? Similarly, isn't it reasonable to conclude that as finite beings, we cannot know an infinite Being's full purposes for everything that happens? Professor of Philosophy Alvin Plantinga illustrates this. Suppose you look for an adult St. Bernard in a tent. Because you don't see one, you reasonably assume that there is no St. Bernard. This is a reasonable conclusion. However, suppose you look for a "no-see-um" (e.g., a gnat) in the tent, but you don't see one. Is it reasonable to assume that it must not be there? Of course not! Keller explains, if you say, "'No, I don't see any 'no-see-ums,' that doesn't mean that there aren't any 'no-see-ums' in there because if there were you couldn't see 'em."[10] Similarly, just because we cannot perceive God's purpose in a situation, that does not mean there isn't one. In fact, it seems much more reasonable to conclude that if you have a God big enough to save you no matter the circumstance, he must also have reasons too big for us to perceive.[11] The approach "*if you . . . then I . . .*" disregards the chasm of knowledge and insight that must exist between the Infinite and the finite.

Inklings of Insight

A turning point in Luke's narrative begins in 23:40. Here Luke focuses on the second criminal, the Roman centurion, and the

---

10. Keller, "With All This Suffering"

11. Keller writes similarly (*Reason for God*, 25): "If you have a God great and transcendent enough to be mad at because he hasn't stopped evil and suffering in the world, then you have (at the same moment) a God great and transcendent enough to have good reasons for allowing it to continue that you can't know."

crowd. Their insight into the person and work of Christ stands in stark contrast to the ignorance we have seen so far.

Up to this point, Jesus has heard nothing but mockery. But suddenly an unexpected voice speaks into the darkness. While the first criminal rails against Jesus, demanding to be saved, the second criminal comes to Jesus's defense. He says three things.

First, he rebukes the other criminal by asking, "Do you not fear God?" (23:40). This question expresses his belief in God's justice: God rewards the righteous and punishes the guilty. In many ways the first criminal is a contemporary person. He believes that no matter what a person does, God should love and embrace him. In fact, his demand to be saved suggests that God is obligated to love at the exclusion of justice. It doesn't matter how heinous his crime was that he is now suffering—God should accept him regardless. But the second criminal contradicts him and says, ". . . we are receiving the due reward of our deeds; but this man has done nothing wrong" (23:41). The second criminal knows that God is loving *and* just.

Theologian Miroslav Volf explains in vivid detail the problem of wanting a god who is nothing but all-loving and all-forgiving:

> I suggest imagining that you are delivering a lecture in a war zone . . . Among your listeners are people whose cities and villages have been first plundered, then burned and leveled to the ground, whose daughters and sisters have been raped, whose fathers and brothers have had their throats slit. The topic of the lecture: a Christian attitude toward violence. The thesis: we should not retaliate since God is perfect noncoercive love. Soon you would discover that it takes the quiet of a suburban home for the birth of the thesis that human nonviolence corresponds to God's refusal to judge. In a scorched land, soaked in the blood of the innocent, it will invariably die.[12]

12. Volf, *Exclusion and Embrace*, 303–304.

Second, not only does the criminal assert that God is just; he also highlights that both he and the other criminal are rightly condemned (23:41). In other words, he admits that he is not a good person—that what is happening to him is right. Whereas Jesus is innocent and does not deserve punishment, the two criminals are guilty and "are receiving the due reward of our deeds" (23:41). This admission of unworthiness—"I do not deserve any kindness from God"—is the key for understanding the criminal's last statement.

Finally, the criminal says, "Jesus, remember me when you come into your kingdom" (23:42).[13] This is a remarkable request given his acknowledgment of both God's righteousness and his own guilt. His request is essentially a cry for mercy: "You're just, so I should be punished. But if it is at all possible—though I have done nothing to deserve such kindness—would you remember me when you come into your kingdom?" In this sense, he expresses the most critical insight into salvation, namely that God saves not according to merit but according to grace. God shows kindness to those who transfer their hope from themselves to Jesus alone. Theologian Herman Bavinck explains:

> All religions seek a way of salvation . . . Unique to the Christian religion is the reality of Jesus Christ and the redemption he brings as fully God's initiative; all other religions seek redemption through human action. However the human problem is conceived, it remains human beings who must satisfy the deity and fulfill its demands or law. All religions or philosophies other than the Christian faith are autosoteric. The biblical

---

13. The name Jesus means "God saves." Throughout the trial and crucifixion, everyone addresses Jesus not by name but by title—"Christ." Professor David Buttrick makes an interesting observation: "Only here is Jesus addressed by his proper name, Jesus, no doubt recalling the angel's words to Mary in Luke's first chapter: 'And you will name him Jesus. He will be great, and will be called the Son of the Most High' (1:31–32)" (*Mystery and the Passion*, 171). This not only underscores the rhetorical construction of Luke's Gospel but also the intended effect thereof. It is here at the cross that we have true insight to who Jesus is.

viewpoint is radically different; salvation is solely a gift of grace.[14]

Jesus responds to the criminal's confession with these comforting words: "Truly, I say to you, today you will be with me in Paradise" (23:43). Jesus's promise is as stunning as the criminal's request. Crucifixion was usually reserved for the worst of criminals. But Jesus says that even the chief of sinners can enter the kingdom of God if he places his ultimate trust in the Son of God. Ironically, it's the religious leaders who remain alienated from God. Because they refuse to see their guilt and continue to boast in their moral achievements, Jesus responds to them with nothing but silence (23:35). In God's kingdom, the law of grace permits the worst to get in and the best to stay out.[15]

Moralists in particular take issue with this. They think it is unfair and even absurd for sinners to receive favor: "He's a criminal deemed worthy of execution by crucifixion! Why does he get Paradise? He's done nothing to deserve it!" But that's what mercy is—unmerited kindness. That's the gospel, God showing kindness to contrite sinners who cast themselves on God's mercy. Jesus, after all, "came not to call the righteous, but sinners" (Mark 2:17); he "came to seek and to save the lost" (Luke 19:10).

Luke continues with this theme of unexpected insight by turning our attention to the Roman centurion. The backdrop is unsettling: "It was now about the sixth hour, and there was darkness over the whole land until the ninth hour, while the sun's light failed" (23:44–45).[16] Standing at the foot of the cross, the centurion is able to hear Jesus's final words, "Father, into your hands I commit my spirit!" (23:46). Sensing the supernatural presence of God and overwhelmed by Jesus's piety, the Roman centurion "praised God, saying, 'Certainly this man was

14. Bavinck, *Reformed Dogmatics*, 485.

15. For an extended meditation on this point, see Keller, *Prodigal God*.

16. As most commentators observe, this cannot be accounted for by "natural" events because Jesus's crucifixion occurred during the Jewish Passover—a time in the moon's orbit when a solar eclipse was impossible.

righteous'" (23:47, my translation). Many standard translations read, "Certainly this man was innocent." The original Greek, however, uses the adjective *dikaios*, which means "righteous, upright, just."[17] This is an important distinction.

While the trial scenes emphasize Jesus's innocence, the present scene highlights his righteousness. Jesus never broke any of God's commandments; hence his innocence. But Jesus also perfectly obeyed the Father, even to the point of death; hence his righteousness. That is why the centurion doesn't simply say, "He died as an innocent man." Luke is making a profound theological point through the mouth of the centurion: Jesus died as a *righteous* person. His account was neither break-even nor red; it was positive because of his perfect obedience.

We are dwelling on this point because it is integral to understanding why the gospel is good news. The apostle Paul writes of Jesus: "For our sake [God] made him to be sin who knew no sin, so that in him we might become the righteousness of God" (2 Corinthians 5:21). On the one hand, the gospel declares that God reckoned our sins to Jesus; hence his death pays for the penalty of our sins. On the other hand, the gospel declares that God reckoned Jesus's righteousness to us; hence his exaltation becomes our glory. By virtue of union with Christ, anyone that trusts in Jesus—criminal, centurion, or chief of sinners—receives the immutable verdict "righteous."

Finally, we see inklings of insight in the crowds. Luke indicates that the crowds "had assembled for this spectacle" (24:48). But "when they saw what had taken place, [they] returned home beating their breasts" (23:48). "Beating their breasts" (23:48) was an expression of repentance. For example, in Luke 18:13 Jesus describes a "tax collector, standing far off, [who] would not even lift up his eyes to heaven, but beat his breast, saying, 'God, be merciful to me, a sinner!'"

17. Laurie Brink observes: "The word and its derivatives occur 14 times within the Gospel (Luke 1:6, 17, 75; 2:25; 5:32; 10:29; 12:57; 14:14; 15:7; 18:9; 20:20; 23:41, 47, 50) and always have the connotation of 'righteous'" (*Soldiers in Luke-Acts*, 106).

Like the centurion, upon witnessing God's supernatural presence and the manner of Jesus's death, the crowds sensed that there was something wrong not just with the situation but also—and perhaps more so—with them.[18] In a mysterious way, the Holy Spirit was working in their hearts to convict them of their guilt and bring them to a place of repentance. This conviction would eventually blossom to full conversion through the apostolic proclamation of the gospel (e.g., Acts 2:14–42). But even now the clouds of ignorance were fading as the Son's glory shone from the cross.

What Makes the Difference?

The inevitable question arises: Why does one criminal repent while the other does not? Why does the one Roman centurion see something different in Jesus while the other soldiers do not? Why do the crowds begin to repent while the religious leaders do not? The gospel maintains that all people are the same, "for all have sinned and fall short of the glory of God" (Romans 3:23). Therefore, the answer does not lie in one group being innately superior or made of better moral fabric. So, again, why do some become enlightened while others remain ignorant?

On the one hand, because "salvation belongs to the Lord" (Psalm 3:8; Jonah 2:9), there is little we can do to change ourselves and others. We cannot develop a program that guarantees conversion. On the other hand, because the Bible speaks both of divine sovereignty *and* human responsibility, there is much we can do. Church historian Chad Van Dixhoorn aptly says: "God is sovereign, but in a very real way we are free, and in

---

18. New Testament professor Heather M. Gorman notes that the crowds at Jesus's crucifixion were likely those at his trial; while the crowds "joined forces with the leaders during the trial before Pilate, they do not remain joined with them until the end. When the rulers mock Jesus at the crucifixion, the people simply watch (23:35) and eventually beat their breasts in remorse for their wrongful condemnation" (*Interweaving Innocence*, 156).

every way we are responsible for our actions."[19] Luke's narrative suggests two things. We can pray earnestly for the advance of the gospel and we can commit to simple presentations of the gospel.

The conversions of the criminal, Roman centurion, and crowds occur after Jesus's prayer in 23:34: "Father, forgive them, for *they know not* what they do." His prayer says implicitly: "They're ignorant, so Father enlighten them." Jesus is asking God to grant these people insight into who he is and why he is dying on the cross. In this way, Luke makes clear that God's salvation goes forth in direct response to prayer. Professor Joan Mueller says it like this:

> After Jesus prays the prayer of forgiveness, the criminal crucified with Jesus asks to be remembered in the kingdom (Luke 23:42). . . The invitation to repentance implicit in the prayer of forgiveness bears fruit in the Roman centurion who praises God and declares Jesus' innocence (23:47). . . The people around the cross return home beating their breasts (23:48) and thus demonstrate the repentance needed for the appropriation of the grace of forgiveness.[20]

The Bible could not be clearer that prayers make a difference. When we look at both the Old and New Testament, whenever salvation goes forth, almost always it is in direct response to prayer. Given this reality, God's sovereignty in salvation cannot become an excuse not to pray. In fact, prayer is one of God's sovereign means for saving people. Theologian John M. Frame explains—and underscores—the necessity of prayer in God's plan of salvation:

> Now, of course, prayer doesn't change the eternal plan of God. But within that eternal plan are many plans for means and ends. God ordains that crops will grow, but not without water and sun. He ordains that people will

19. Van Dixhoorn, *Confessing the Faith*, 45.
20. Mueller, *Is Forgiveness Possible?*, 51.

be saved, but (ordinarily) not without the teaching of the Word. And he ordains that we will have everything we truly need, but not without prayer. God's eternal plan has determined that many things will be achieved by prayer and that many things will not be achieved without prayer.[21]

Perhaps no one spoke more strongly about God's sovereignty than the apostle Paul. For example, in Ephesians 1:4–5 he wrote: "[God] chose us in [Christ] before the foundation of the world. . . In love, he predestined us for adoption as sons through Jesus Christ, according to the purpose of his will." At the same time, few people more regularly asked for prayer than the apostle: "Finally, brothers, pray for us, that the word of the Lord may speed ahead and be honored, as happened among you" (2 Thessalonians 3:1). Paul believed in God's sovereignty and in human responsibility, especially as that is expressed in prayer.

What has the power to move people toward insight? What can soften hardened hearts and bring even the most hostile to a place of contrition and repentance? Luke indicates that prayer is one of God's ordinary means for accomplishing extraordinary things.

In addition to prayer, a plain presentation of the gospel is instrumental in moving people to repent. Here too the apostle Paul is helpful: "And I, when I came to you, brothers, did not come proclaiming to you the testimony of God with lofty speech or wisdom. For I decided to know nothing among you except Jesus Christ and him crucified" (1 Corinthians 2:1–2).

Indeed, it is Christ crucified that leads the second criminal, the Roman centurion, and the crowds to repentance and insight. Like the religious leaders and Roman soldiers, some claim today that they will believe in God if they witness a miracle or hear a persuasive argument. The Bible, however, reiterates that it is a plain presentation of the gospel—namely that Christ died for sinners—that changes people. "Jews demand signs and

---

21. Frame, *Systematic Theology*, 1054.

Greeks seek wisdom, but we preach Christ crucified, a stumbling block to Jews and folly to Gentiles, but to those who are called . . . [we preach] Christ the power of God and the wisdom of God" (1 Corinthians 1:22–24).

A powerful illustration of this comes from the early ministry of Billy Graham. In 1955 he received an invitation to preach at Cambridge University. Aware of his modest theological education and intimidated by the refined university students, Graham considered cancelling the event. In the end he accepted the invitation but deviated from his usual pattern of presenting the gospel in simple ways. To appeal to the intellectual elite, he checkered his sermons with pedantic material. And for the first two days nothing happened. Reflecting years later on what took place before his third presentation, Graham wrote:

> Then, on my knees with a deep sense of failure, inadequacy, and helplessness, I turned to God. My gift, such as it was, was not to present the intellectual side of the Gospel. I knew that. What those students needed was a clear understanding of the simple but profound truths of the Gospel: our separation from God because of sin; Christ's provision of forgiveness and new life; and our hope because of Him.[22]

Graham repented. He admitted that he was seeking to please the audience rather than God, that he was trusting in sophisticated argumentation rather than the simple gospel message. The next night he set aside his original sermon and presented the gospel in his usual basic manner. Graham summarized the results. "That night more than 400 Cambridge students stayed behind to make their commitment to Christ. . . For the rest of the week, I strove to be as simple and yet as direct as possible, and the response continued to surprise us all."[23]

22. Graham, *Just As I Am*, 259.

23. Ibid. Here it's worth noting the story of Louis Zamperini, a World War II veteran, prisoner of war, and survivor of Japanese labor camps. His astonishing journey is told in Laura Hillenbrand's *Unbroken*. The Hollywood movie of

It is worthwhile to reiterate that conversion is a mysterious and supernatural work. In the end, only God can change lives. Yet, divine sovereignty does not preclude human responsibility. We can—indeed we must—pray for the progress of the gospel and preach the basic message of Christ crucified for sinners. Through these ordinary means, God will accomplish his divine purpose of drawing people into a relationship with himself.

You Never Know

One final remark is in order. Consider who converts—a notorious criminal, a hardened centurion, a callous crowd. Who would have thought? And that's exactly the point. You never know. A person can change from being a persecutor of the church to a champion of the gospel. To be sure, like the Jewish leaders, Roman soldiers, and railing criminal, many will hear the gospel, laugh, raise objections, and walk away. But others will respond with faith and repentance. You never know. Our only responsibility is to invite all to come, see, taste, and know the Lord is good.

---

the same name stops short of Zamperini's remarkable and life-changing conversion to Christianity. The final chapter and epilogue of Louie Zamperini's biography tell of a life that was forever transformed through an invitation to hear a simple gospel presentation (by Billy Graham!). Louie himself began working in a church and inviting others to come and see Christ (see 378–84, 389–91).

3

The King Rises

Luke 23:50—24:12

"WHY DO YOU SEEK the living among the dead?" (24:5). The angels' question startles the women at Jesus's tomb; and, though two thousand years have passed, their question continues to startle us today. In this chapter, we consider three points related to this question: the reality of the resurrection, the necessity of the resurrection, and the consequence of the resurrection.

He Is Not Among the Dead

Luke leaves no doubt that Jesus actually died. A man named Joseph from the Jewish town of Arimathea "went to Pilate and asked for the body of Jesus. Then he took it down and wrapped it in a linen shroud and laid him in a tomb cut in stone, where no one had ever yet been laid" (23:52–53). Joseph would not have asked for Jesus's body if he were still alive. Also, the removal of Jesus's corpse was no small endeavor. The spikes driven through Jesus's hands and feet had to be removed. Then the deadweight of Jesus's body had to be supported as it was lowered to the ground. Finally, his body had to be wrapped in a linen shroud and placed in a tomb. If Jesus were still alive, surely someone would have noticed.

Some skeptics propose that Jesus merely fainted and later awoke (or was revived) in the tomb. This idea, commonly known as the "swoon theory," has many problems. Author Hank Hanegraaff notes:

> It would entail believing that Jesus survived three days without medical attention, single-handedly rolled away an enormously heavy tombstone, subdued an armed guard, strolled around on pierced feet, and seduced his disciples into communicating the myth that he had conquered death while he lived out the remainder of his pathetic life in obscurity.[1]

It is easier to believe that Jesus died (and was resurrected) than to believe that he merely fainted and was resuscitated.

But Luke also leaves no doubt that Jesus actually rose from the dead. The very women who had witnessed his crucifixion (23:49) "went to the tomb" on Sunday morning (24:1) but "did not find the body of the Lord Jesus" (24:3). Understandably, the women "were perplexed about this" (24:4), and so the angels explained: "He is not here, but has risen" (24:6). The women now had to face the reality not just of his death but also of his resurrection.

Common Objections to the Resurrection

Jesus's resurrection rubs against the contemporary mind. Professor Richard Hays writes:

> The New Testament's accounts of the resurrection of Jesus have proven particularly problematic for modern interpreters. Stories about the resurrection of a man crucified, dead, and buried contradict everything that orthodox post-Enlightenment historians take to be

---

1. Hanegraaff, *Resurrection*, 20.

axiomatic about the nature of history and the reality in which we live.[2]

But the resurrection isn't just a "modern" problem. Even Jesus's own disciples did not believe it at first. This is important to highlight because many today believe that first-century people were unenlightened and willing to believe anything. But that idea is mistaken. Professor Stephen T. Davis observes:

> For one thing, we need to remind ourselves that the disciples were convinced that Jesus had truly died. And contrary to the claims of some twentieth-century theologians (who make it sound as if first-century folk were almost pantingly eager to believe in resurrection and other miracles, and would do so at the drop of a hat), they were as convinced as we are that dead people stay dead. They were definitely not expecting to encounter Jesus.[3]

When Jesus's disciples heard the women's report, "these words seemed to them an idle tale, and they did not believe them" (24:11).[4] In other words, the first disciples responded exactly the way we would today. There is no suggestion in the narrative that the disciples had any predisposition or prior commitment to believe that Jesus would be raised.

In his book *The Resurrection of the Son of God*, Wright demonstrates that Jesus's contemporaries, both Jews and Greco-Romans, would have been just as skeptical—if not more so—than people today about his resurrection. Jews believed in a general resurrection—the renewal of all things, but not in an "isolated" resurrection. Wright comments, "nobody imagined

---

2. Hays, "Reading Scripture," 216.

3. Davis, "'Seeing' the Risen Christ," 136.

4. C. Franklin Brookhart's comments are spot on: "The major factor we need to note here is that doubt is a category introduced by the New Testament itself into the resurrection accounts... Who could not be shocked at the degree of open honesty in this account? And again, the apostles are, surprisingly, the ones who appear to doubt most strongly" (*Living the Resurrection*, 58–59).

that any individual had already been raised, or would be raised in advance of the great last day."[5] Therefore, the disciples would have found it difficult to believe in a *single* resurrection in history.[6] Similarly, no thoughtful Greco-Roman person would have been predisposed to embrace the message of Jesus's bodily resurrection. According to Greco-Roman thought, the body was bad, the soul good; salvation was conceived in terms of the soul's liberation from the body.[7] Therefore, the idea of a bodily resurrection would have been alien to their worldview.

Another common objection to the resurrection is that the Gospel accounts are fabrications which the early church leaders invented in order to legitimize their authority. Recalling his own skepticism, homicide detective J. Warner Wallace explains:

> When I was an atheist, I recognized that the most significant claim of the alleged apostolic *eyewitnesses* was their claim related to the resurrection. . . I always assumed it was a lie. Maybe it was just my skeptical nature or my prior experience with people on the job. I understand the capacity people have to lie when it serves their purposes. In my view, the apostles were no different. In an effort to promote their cause and strengthen their own position within their religious community, I believed these twelve men concocted, executed, and maintained the most elaborate and influential conspiracy of all time.[8]

There are two problems, however, with this objection.

The first is that Luke goes out of his way to give the names and background information of the witnesses to Jesus's death

---

5. Wright, *Resurrection of the Son of God*, 205.

6. Davidson, *Birth of the Church*, 16: "Even for the majority of Palestinian Jews who, unlike the Sadducees, professed hope in the resurrection, the idea was bizarre. . . The notion that a person had been raised bodily from the tomb while history was still going on would have seemed almost as strange to first-century Jews as it does to most Western people today."

7. See Keller, *Reason for God*, 215.

8. Wallace, *Cold-Case Christianity*, 113.

and resurrection. He not only names Joseph but also details where he was from, his occupation, and his religious beliefs (23:50–51). Later Luke gives the precise identities of the women who went to the tomb (24:10). Why are these details so important? Suppose I say, "Yesterday, I had coffee with Whitney Houston!" You object, "That can't be. She has passed away, and even if she were alive, why would she have coffee with you?" I respond, "Our friend David was there, too. And so was your sister Jennifer. And so was Ricky from our intramural football league." If each person verifies my story, you are forced to at least reconsider your skepticism. Writing only a few decades after the Christ's resurrection, Luke included personal details because he wanted his readers to verify his account by speaking to the living witnesses.[9]

Such witnesses included women: "Now it was Mary Magdalene and Joanna and Mary the mother of James and the other women with them who told these things to the apostles" (24:10). This raises the other major problem with the objection that the church invented the resurrection story. Had the early church wanted to fabricate the story, they would have made men the first witnesses. In the first-century Mediterranean world, women had low social status and could not serve as witnesses in court. Scholar Robert Karl Gnuse notes:

> In that ancient age the testimony of women was not recognized as being significant, certainly not in trial situations. To affirm them as the first to testify to the resurrection of Jesus was an incredible thing for the

---

9. Keller argues along similar lines in his comments on 1 Corinthians 15:3–6: "Paul's letter was to a church, and therefore it was a public document, written to be read aloud. Paul was inviting anyone who doubted that Jesus had appeared to people after his death to go and talk to the eyewitnesses if they wished. It was a bold challenge and one that could easily be taken up, since during the *pax Romana* travel around the Mediterranean was safe and easy. Paul could not have made such a challenge if those eyewitnesses didn't exist" (*Reason for God*, 204).

ancient church to recall and for the Gospel writers to
record.[10]

Given all this, why does Luke name women as the primary witnesses? The only reasonable conclusion we can draw is that the
church must have maintained the original accounts because
they represented what in fact had taken place.

He Had to Die and He Had to Rise

The angels go on to explain why the women should have expected a resurrected Jesus: "Remember how he told you, while he was
still in Galilee, that the Son of Man *must* be delivered into the
hands of sinful men and be crucified and on the third day rise"
(24:6–7). The women should have known that Jesus's trial, death,
and resurrection were not random events. Jesus had repeatedly
told his followers that his betrayal, death, *and* resurrection were
all necessary to accomplish God's plan of salvation.

There is a tension that runs throughout the entire Bible. On
the one hand, because God is holy and just, he cannot overlook
sin. Divine justice demands atonement for sin. On the other
hand, because God is merciful and loving, he does not want us
to suffer the penalty of our sins. The remedy for this quandary
was God giving his only beloved Son to die in our place and to
satisfy divine justice. In this sense, Jesus *had* to die.

The resurrection, however, indicates that God's justice has
been satisfied. It has been executed in full; there is no more sin
to punish. "[T]he resurrection of Jesus is the validating event
that affirms once and for all that Jesus's sacrifice was acceptable
to God and nothing more needed to be done to bring us into relationship with him."[11] The resurrection is God's cosmic receipt

10. Gnuse, *Trajectories of Justice*, 97–98. Jo Kadlecek similarly observes that
not only was the report of Jesus's resurrection "the last thing they expected,"
but "they certainly did not expect to hear it from the most unlikely witnesses
in Jerusalem" (*Desperate Faith*, 36).

11. Miller, *Did Jesus Really Rise from the Dead?*, 164.

showing that all our sins have been paid in full. This is why the angels basically say to the women, "Don't you remember that Jesus had to die for you? And don't you realize that he also had to be raised to life? If he were still among the dead, that would mean God's wrath continues!"

At first glance all this sounds unduly theological and otherwise inconsequential. But in the New Testament the verb "remember" (24:6, 8) means much more than mere recollection of facts. It has a spiritual sense relating to identity and purpose. For instance, James 1:23–24 reads: "For if anyone is a hearer of the word and not a doer, he is like a man who looks intently at his natural face in a mirror. For he looks at himself and goes away and at once forgets what he was like." Similarly, in the Old Testament, repeated references to remembering God and his mercy, expressed especially in the exodus, relate to vocation: the Israelites were to remember their unique identity as a redeemed people called to reflect God's mercy and glory to all the nations. In this sense, when the angels exhort the women to "remember" Jesus's words, and when the women finally "remembered," Luke has in view the basic category of identity: they are to take hold of a new identity and purpose that are rooted in the death and resurrection of Christ.

When you come to personally believe in the necessity of Christ's death and resurrection, you change in at least two ways. First, you experience freedom from bitterness. On the one hand, in the trial and death of Jesus, the Bible acknowledges that we live in a world where things are not the way they are supposed to be.[12] Disease, injustice, and death are wrong, not merely figments of our imagination. On the other hand, the Bible teaches that even victims are perpetrators of injustice and contributors to the world's brokenness. The gospel says that to some degree all share in the very sins they despise. This is, of course, difficult

12. This phrase is adapted from the title of Plantinga Jr's *Not the Way It's Supposed to Be*.

to admit. J. D. Vance comments in his *New York Times* bestseller *Hillbilly Elegy*:

> We tend to overstate and to understate, to glorify the good and ignore the bad in ourselves. This is why the folks of Appalachia reacted strongly to an honest look at some of its most impoverished people. . . and it's why I spent the first eighteen years of my life pretending that everything in the world was a problem except me. The truth is hard, and the hardest truths for hill people are the ones they must tell about themselves.[13]

If we remain "convinced that any crimes we have committed are the result of adverse circumstances" and refuse to see "ourselves as criminals who have broken God's law," we will never break free from bitterness.[14] But if we admit that we have failed to love God and have fallen short of the standards we impose on others, we cease to see ourselves solely as victims. We see that we are part of the reason why Jesus had to come to die and rise for sinners. This basic insight is the first step toward gospel-freedom.

A poignant example of such freedom is found in Victor Hugo's novel *Les Misérables*. The protagonist Jean Valjean spirals into bitterness after repeated experiences of injustice and poverty. But at a pivotal moment of grace he sees that not only has he been hurt by the sins of others, but that he too has sinned against others. His anger ebbs in the freedom of forgiveness and service.

> As he wept, daylight penetrated more and more clearly into his soul; an extraordinary light; a light at once ravishing and terrible. His past life, his first fault, his long expiation, his external brutishness, his internal hardness, his dismissal to liberty, rejoicing in manifold plans of vengeance, what had happened to him at the Bishop's, the last thing that he had done, that theft of forty sous from a child, a crime all the more cowardly,

---

13. Vance, *Hillbilly Elegy*, 20.
14. Velotta, *Reclaiming Victory*, 179.

and all the more monstrous since it had come after the Bishop's pardon,—all this recurred to his mind and appeared clearly to him, but with a clearness which he had never hitherto witnessed. He examined his life, and it seemed horrible to him; his soul, and it seemed frightful to him. In the meantime a gentle light rested over this life and this soul.[15]

Second, when we believe that Jesus had to die and rise for us, we experience the freedom that comes from being radically loved. That Jesus had to die for our sins reminds us of our failures. We rebelled against God's lordship and strayed after false gods, seeking security and meaning in them instead of the one true and living God. But Jesus's death for our sins also reminds us of God's amazing love: he loved rebellious and adulterous people enough to give up his only Son for their sake. Reflecting on this twin-reality, Paul concludes: "God shows his love for us in that while we were still sinners, Christ died for us. . . For if while we were enemies we were reconciled to God by the death of his Son, much more, now that we are reconciled, shall we be saved by his life" (Romans 5: 8, 10). In other words, if God loved us when we were rebels and adulterers, how much more so now that we have been made children of God and citizens of his kingdom?

So much of life is devoted to trying to win the love, acceptance, and approval of others. C. S. Lewis said it best:

> You discover gradually, in almost indefinable ways, that [an Inner Circle] exists and that you are outside it, and then later, perhaps, that you are inside it. . . It is not easy, even at a given moment, to say who is inside and who is outside. Some people are obviously in and some are obviously out, but there are always several on the border line. . . From inside it may be designated, in simple cases, by mere enumeration; it may be called "you and Tony and me." . . . From outside, if you have

15. Hugo, *Les Misérables*, I.II.VIII.

despaired of getting into it, you call it "that gang" or
"they" or "so-and-so and his set" or "the Caucus" or
"the Inner Ring." . . . you have met the phenomenon of
an Inner Ring.[16]

The desire to become a part of an "Inner Ring" is, in one sense,
natural. The problem, however, is that often people cease to be
people and instead becomes means for advancing our social
agenda. Moreover, we become Great Pretenders; like Jacob
we clothe ourselves with another's attire to hear words of af-
fection from those who would never love our "true selves"
(Genesis 27). "Of all passions the passion for the Inner Ring is
most skillful in making a man who is not yet a very bad man
do very bad things."[17]

The gospel checks such "passion for the Inner Ring" by
telling us: Stop seeking acceptance because you have already
been accepted in Jesus Christ; stop seeking love because you
have been loved to give love; stop pretending to be perfect because you are perfect in him; stop pursuing good works to atone
for past sins or to merit future favor because all your sins have
been paid for in the death and resurrection of the Son. In sum,
God's radical love in Christ frees us from wanting too much to
be in an "Inner Ring" by reminding us that we are already in *the*
Inner Ring: "indeed our fellowship is with the Father and with
his Son Jesus Christ" (1 John 1:3).

Resurrection Life

So far we have considered the historicity and necessity of the
resurrection: it actually happened and it had to happen. Now
we come to our final point—the new reality ushered in by the
resurrection. You may believe in the historicity and necessity of
the resurrection. But do you live as if Jesus were still among the

16. Lewis, *Weight of Glory*, 143–45.
17. Ibid., 152–53.

dead? Has the reality of the resurrection led to new life? Has it resulted in tangible and profound change?

Today many people view Jesus as a source of inspiration, a model of virtue, a teacher *par excellence*, but nothing more. The women at the tomb had this perspective. They did not go to Jesus's tomb expecting to encounter the risen Lord. Like many today, they believed that Jesus had been a commendable teacher. That's all.

Luke's Gospel, however, does not allow for this sort of benign perspective. Luke maintains that the eternal Son of God entered into the world as a human being, died as the only mediator between God and man, and was resurrected to conquer sin and death. If the Easter message is not true—if Jesus did not rise from the dead—everything he claimed and taught is a matter of personal preference. We can embrace or reject whatever we please because he was nothing but a human teacher. But if the Easter message is true—if Jesus did rise from the dead—his staggering claim to be God is true. Keller comments:

> Sometimes people approach me and say, "I really struggle with this aspect of Christian teaching. I like this part of Christian belief, but I don't think I can accept that part." I usually respond: "If Jesus rose from the dead, then you have to accept all he said; if he didn't rise from the dead, then why worry about any of what he said? The issue on which everything hangs is not whether or not you like his teaching but whether or not he rose from the dead."[18]

We must live differently now that the king has risen.

Moreover, if the resurrection of Jesus happened, everything falls into proper perspective. Cancer, unemployment, and even death are no longer the final word. Jesus has risen! And because his resurrection is our resurrection, our final word is glory unending.

18. Keller, *Reason for God*, 202.

In his book *Rejoicing in Lament*, J. Todd Billings details his battle with cancer. When he first received his diagnosis, his life fell apart. "My 'world' seemed to be caving in on itself with fog in each direction I turned, so that no light could shine in."[19] But then he began to meditate on the resurrection and came to the conclusion: "God's story does not annihilate my cancer story, but it does envelop and redefine it. Indeed, it asks for my story to be folded into the dying and rising of Christ as one who belongs to him."[20] We can—and ought to—grieve when cancer breaks down our bodies and families; the resurrection does not make us stoics. But we dare "not grieve as others do who have no hope" (1 Thessalonians 4:13). Because of the resurrection, even our weeping is filled with joy.

The resurrection effects real change because it really happened and because we really are forgiven and counted righteous in Christ. Resurrection-life is not wishful living. "The Christian understanding of hope . . . is not . . . optimism. Optimism often connotes a blind inevitability that all will be well, regardless of the evidence that might say otherwise."[21] Resurrection-life is about pursuing a new life rooted in the historical and theological realities accomplished in the death and resurrection of the Son. Belief in the historicity and necessity of the resurrection demands new rhythms of life.

A comparison of Luke's Gospel and Acts shows how much the resurrection changed the disciples. Everything changed—their company, their ambition, their guilt. Before the resurrection, the disciples associated only with Jews. After the resurrection, the disciples lived in new and diverse communities, breaking the traditional boundaries of race, class, and even religion. Before the resurrection, the disciples pursued power and prestige. Regularly they would bicker about who would be the greatest in Jesus's kingdom. After the resurrection, they did

19. Billings, *Rejoicing in Lament*, 1.

20. Ibid., 169.

21. Doran, *Hope in the Age of Climate Change*, 60.

not care about status but aspired to become servants like their master. Before the resurrection, the disciples were self-confident individuals who ultimately abandoned Jesus in his time of greatest need. After the resurrection, they were self-forgetful, forgiven, and courageous persons willing to suffer persecution and death for the sake of the gospel.

The New Testament records various conversion accounts that illustrate the profound change that belief in the resurrection brings. One of the better-known accounts is that of the apostle Paul who encountered Jesus on the road to Damascus. He was blinded by the encounter but—ironically—saw clearly for the first time that the person he was persecuting is the Son of God. After regaining sight, he was baptized, joined the community of disciples, and "immediately he proclaimed Jesus in the synagogues, saying, 'He is the Son of God'" (Acts 9:18–20). Paul had been wrong; he had treated Jesus as if he were still among the dead. His mistake was consequential, resulting in the first systematic persecution of the church. But so too was his repentance. It was not so much that Paul suddenly sought to live a radical life based on a commitment to be countercultural. More positively, he made it his ambition to conform to the new reality ushered in by the reality and significance of Christ's resurrection. His change serves as a paradigm for the way life must change because of the resurrection.

"He is risen, he is risen indeed!" Everything is different now. It cannot be otherwise.

4

The King Accompanies
Luke 24:13–35

THE SECOND RESURRECTION APPEARANCE recorded by Luke takes place on the road to Emmaus. Two disciples are walking along this road on a Sunday afternoon. Only a few hours earlier, they were grieving Jesus's death when suddenly some of the women rushed in to tell the disciples he has risen. Despite hearing this news, however, these two do not believe. They have lost hope and are moving on with their lives.

Along the seven-mile journey, the risen Jesus "drew near and went with them" (24:15). The narrative raises three important questions. First, these two disciples do not recognize him. Why not? Second, these disciples are downcast. Why? Third, the two disciples eventually recognize Jesus. How?

Why Can't the Disciples Recognize Jesus?

The seven-mile walk is slow enough for extended interaction. When Jesus asks about the events in Jerusalem, "they stood still, looking sad" (24:17). This detail is important for understanding the amount of time Jesus spends walking with them. It takes about fifteen minutes to walk a mile. But now, not only do you have to account for the fact that they've stopped walking, they are also very somber and reflective, slowing their pace to a dejected sulk. After asking his question, Jesus explains everything the Old Testament says about him: "And beginning with Moses and all the Prophets, he interpreted to them in all the Scriptures the things concerning himself" (24:27). Author William H. Shepherd Jr. says: "Luke makes sure we know that the lesson is comprehensive: it covers the entire span of the Hebrew Bible."[1] This is at least a half-day discussion.

Yet, despite this lengthy time together, the two disciples do not recognize Jesus. "One of the great conundrums of Luke's account is why the disciples didn't recognize Jesus."[2] Why is this the case?

At first thinking that the man who joined them on the road is an uninformed "visitor to Jerusalem" (24:18), the two begin to tell him who Jesus was, or rather who they had hoped he would be. Their words indicate that they had longed for someone extraordinary. They describe Jesus as "a prophet mighty in deed and word" (24:19). They go on to share, "we had hoped that he was the one to redeem Israel" (24:21). In sum, they had hoped Jesus would be an extraordinary warrior who would restore King David's glory.[3] They had been looking for a Samson, a Goliath, not an ordinary carpenter. Perhaps all the more so now that there were rumors of his resurrection. Surely a resurrected Jesus would be even more glorious!

This bias toward the extraordinary is why all the characters so far have failed to recognize Jesus. At Jesus's trial Pilate and Herod were looking for an extraordinary king, not a man who suffers with and for his people. At the crucifixion the Jewish

---

1. Shepherd Jr., *If a Sermon Falls in the Forest . . .*, 74.

2. Woodward, Gooder, and Pryce, *Journeying with Luke*, 68.

3. Carson, "Who is This 'Son of God'?": "The two disciples on the Emmaus road had hoped that Jesus 'was the one who was going to redeem Israel' (Luke 24:21), that is, they hoped he was the long-awaited Davidic king. In this expectation, however, they had no category for a crucified Davidic king, a crucified Messiah."

leaders, Roman soldiers, and first criminal were looking for an extraordinary display of power, not a man dying in shame and weakness. Now on the road to Emmaus the two disciples are looking for an extraordinary Savior, not an ordinary man walking with other ordinary men. They couldn't recognize Jesus because of their preconceived idea of what the messiah should look like.[4]

In J. R. R. Tolkien's *The Lord of the Rings*, the wizard Gandalf the Grey resurrects as Gandalf the White; he is upgraded with more powers and a more celestial appearance. We may be tempted to think that the resurrected Jesus experienced a similar kind of upgrade and became so dazzling that he couldn't have been missed. Such expectations of post-resurrection splendor are found in ancient documents. For example, *The Gospel of Peter* describes the resurrected Jesus as a magnificent giant so huge that his head reached the clouds. The resurrected Jesus of this particular "Gospel" is everything we would expect. But Luke's narrative continues to oppose such grandiosity.[5] The resurrected Jesus was easy to miss because he was far too ordinary.

Today, many hold similar expectations of Jesus. They say that they will believe if they experience him in an extraordinary way. They want to hear a voice, see a vision, witness a miracle.

---

4. This illustrates well how our presuppositions—the prior commitments and conclusions that we bring to the table when assessing situations—impact what we see. Wallace writes: "All of us hold presuppositions that can impact the way we see the world around us. . . It sounds simple, but our presuppositions are sometimes hidden in a way that makes them hard to uncover and recognize" (*Cold-Case Christianity*, 24). Similar to the two disciples, Wallace goes on to admit his own failure to recognize the risen Jesus: "When I was an atheist, I held many presuppositions that tainted the way I investigated the claims of Christianity. . . I was committed to the notion that we would ultimately find a *natural* answer for everything we once thought to be *supernatural*" (ibid., 25).

5. As William Lane Craig puts it, to appreciate the ordinariness of Luke's Gospel, "you only have to read the account in the apocryphal Gospel of Peter, which describes Jesus' triumphant exit from the tomb as a gigantic figure whose head reaches above the clouds, supported by giant angels, followed by a talking cross, heralded by a voice from heaven, and all witnessed by a Roman guard, the Jewish leaders, and a multitude of spectators" (*On Guard*, 227).

Luke's Gospel, however, suggests that an encounter with God will often be quite ordinary. Kim V. Engelmann writes:

> There is a certain divine delight in the ordinary . . . a certain desire on the part of God to engage with us *in the ordinary*, because this is the nature of love—to meet others in their world and delight in it with unselfish participation. Thus Jesus' desire to be included in the disciples' ordinary conversation on the Emmaus Road is the epitome of God saying, "Let me into the ordinariness of your life, into all of it—from the conversations to the dusty walk to the questions to a simple supper—all of it." God loves the ordinary and uses ordinary people and ordinary life to make himself visible. This is the message of the Emmaus Road.[6]

Sometimes when people give testimonies of their conversion to Christianity, their stories are dramatic and striking. To be sure, God sometimes works in extraordinary ways, but this is uncommon. Given this, it is interesting that testimonies of instantaneous and radical transformations tend to receive special attention. Such preferential treatment can promote a warped view of the way God works, leading us to expect that God prefers the extraordinary over the ordinary.[7]

---

6. Engelmann, *Soul-Shaping Small Groups*, 72.

7. This preference for the extraordinary is reflected in the essay "Why the Resurrection is Unbelievable" by Dr. Richard Carrier, an atheist. Carrier argues that "extraordinary claims require extraordinary evidence" (298). His argument goes like this: since we would need extraordinary evidence to prove that "I own an interstellar spacecraft," how much more evidence would we need to substantiate "the claim that Jesus arose from the dead"? (ibid., 299). Jesus's resurrection, says Carrier, "is an extraordinary claim, and thus requires extraordinary evidence—more evidence, even, than I would need to convince you I own an interstellar spacecraft" (ibid.). In conclusion, he says: "None of the evidence is extraordinary enough to justify believing an extraordinary explanation. All the evidence we have is ordinary and has ordinary explanations. In fact, those ordinary explanations actually explain the evidence better" (ibid., 307). But that is precisely Luke's point: God reveals the extraordinary in the ordinary.

Perhaps you have heard this illustration of a man facing torrential floods. He prayed, "God, rescue me!" Before the flood-waters came, the man's neighbor asked him if he wanted a ride out of town. The man refused: "No thank you. I prayed to God to rescue me, and I know he will." So the neighbor drove off. As the floodwaters began to rise, a rescue boat came, and the people urged him to get in: "It's only going to get worse! Come on!" But the man refused: "No thank you. I prayed to God to rescue me, and I know he will." So the rescue boat left. The floodwaters continued to rise, and the man took refuge on the roof of his home. A helicopter came, and through a megaphone the rescuers yelled, "This is your last chance! Take hold of the ladder!" Again the man refused: "No thank you. I prayed to God to rescue me, and I know he will." So the helicopter flew off. The floodwaters continued to rise until the man finally drowned. When he appeared before God, he protested, "Why didn't you rescue me?" God responded: "You fool! I sent you a car, a boat, and a helicopter, and you refused my help all three times!"

Like that unfortunate man, the two disciples on the road to Emmaus are blinded by their preference for an "extraordinary" Savior.

If you are exploring Christianity, I hope the Emmaus encounter encourages you. God reveals himself in ordinary ways. Perhaps God is already working in your life through ordinary relationships—friends, coworkers, and family members who love Christ. Jesus may be much nearer to you than you realize, already speaking to you, addressing your concerns, and answering your prayers. Perhaps what is needed is not extraordinary revelations but an appreciation for the ordinary means of grace.

Why Are the Disciples Downcast?

"On the ironic journey to Emmaus living disciples talk about a dead Jesus, while a living Jesus speaks with lifeless disciples."[8]

8. Edwards, *Gospel According to Luke*, 720.

Why are they downcast? Luke provides two reasons. The first is obvious, the second less so.

First, the two disciples are despondent because they lack "resurrection faith." New Testament scholar Jack Dean Kingsbury writes: ". . . the sadness and hopelessness that have overtaken the two disciples ultimately stem from the fact that they do not believe that Jesus has been raised from the dead."[9] This unbelief, in turn, forces them to confront the inevitability of their own deaths and the inescapable sense of meaningless that follows.

In his discussion on Jesus's resurrection, the apostle Paul says, "If the dead are not raised, 'Let us eat and drink, for tomorrow we die'" (1 Corinthians 15:32). In other words, if there is no resurrection, no hope of renewal and redemption, it doesn't matter what you do. Why waste life trying to do good when none of it matters in the end? That is the logical conclusion of a life devoid of resurrection faith. In the end, if we came from nothing and return to nothing, no one will remember what we did, and no one will care because no one will be alive to care. If death is all there is, life becomes inescapably cold and meaningless. Death without resurrection is the ultimate leveler of all hope, meaning, and purpose.[10] That is the reality the two disciples confront.

As his death approached, Steve Jobs drew a similar conclusion: "I saw my life as an arch, and that it would end. And

9. Kingsbury, *Conflict in Luke*, 134.

10. Keller explains: "Let's just say you decide you're going to live a very compassionate life. Let's just say this person over here decides they're going to live a life of violence and oppression. Don't you realize, in the end, when you die, you rot? 'Ah, yes, well, but your deeds live on.' Yeah, for a little while. But don't you realize, the three or four billion years in which organic life is going to live on this planet is just an eye blink, just an infinitesimal moment in relationship to the oceans of dead time that precede and come after? In the end, the universe is going to burn up. In the end, nothing is going to make any difference. . . [I]f you're about to die in five minutes, hugging or mugging makes no difference. In other words, your life becomes meaningless. But don't you realize you're going to die in five minutes, so to speak, anyway? And so will the whole world, and so will the whole universe, and so will the whole civilization" ("Reason for Living").

compared to that, nothing mattered, you know. I mean, you're born alone. You're going to die alone, and does anything else really matter?"[11] Joseph Conrad's novel *Heart of Darkness* also portrays the hopelessness of death without resurrection faith. As the once civilized and proper Mr. Kurtz faces his impending death, the narrator Marlow describes his final moments: "I saw on that ivory face the expression . . . of craven terror—of an intense and hopeless despair. . . He cried in a whisper at some image, at some vision,—he cried out twice, a cry that was no more than a breath—'The horror! The horror!'"[12] Even worse, as the book concludes Marlow forces himself to lie in order to preserve a semblance of hope. When Mr. Kurtz's widow asks him to repeat her husband's final words, he says: "I pulled myself together and spoke slowly. 'The last word he pronounced was—your name.'"[13] Conrad's point is Luke's point: if the brutalities of life merely culminate in death, not only is there ultimate darkness, but we also have to lie to ourselves and others in order to create meaning.

Second, Cleopas and the other disciple are downcast because their immediate need has become their ultimate need. Pastor David Stephenson explains that this situation happens "when something that should be peripheral becomes essential, when something that is superficial becomes substantial, when something that is temporal becomes eternal, when something that is secondary becomes primary."[14] In the case of the two dis-

---

11. Isaacson, "Steve Jobs, part 2." As told by biographer Walter Isaacson in a *60 Minutes* interview, Jobs also said: "Sometimes I believe in God, sometimes I don't. I think it's fifty-fifty maybe. But ever since I've had cancer, I've been thinking about it more, and I find myself believing a bit more. Maybe it's because I want to believe in an afterlife, that when you die, it doesn't just all disappear, the wisdom you've accumulated, somehow it lives on. . . but sometimes I think it's just like an on/off switch. *Click!* And you're gone. . . And that's why I don't like putting on/off switches on Apple devices" (ibid.).

12. Conrad, *Heart of Darkness*, 177–78.

13. Ibid., 186.

14. Stephenson, "Gospel in Life." Adapted from Lloyd-Jones, *Setting Our Affections Upon Glory*, 23–26.

ciples, their immediate need is political freedom: "But we had hoped that he was the one to redeem Israel" (24:21).[15] Obviously, this immediate need was not unimportant. The problem was that it had become their ultimate need. The Bible refers to this "exchange" as idolatry, which is when "the human heart takes good things . . . and turns them into ultimate things."[16]

The consequences of this exchange are not to be taken lightly. In the case of the two disciples, happiness is now impossible because the religious leaders had dashed their ultimate hope by killing their prophet (24:19). Moreover, idolatry keeps us from appreciating how our real need for forgiveness and salvation has been met in Christ. A child obsessing over his broken toy cannot appreciate the grand vacation his father has planned for him. In a similar sense, a preoccupation with political freedom inhibits one from realizing—and reveling in—the spiritual freedom Jesus has accomplished by his death and resurrection. Rightly so, Jesus rebukes the disciples with the words, "O foolish ones . . ." (24:25). In effect he was saying: "You fools—you want so little! All you want is freedom from political tyranny when I have come to give you freedom from sin and death!"

Freedom, intimacy, security—all these are good desires. But Luke invites his readers to ask: "Has your good desire become your ultimate desire?" If so, Luke warns us to watch out. When you don't get what you want, you will be crushed. And, perhaps even worse, when you do get what you want, you will also be crushed. Columnist Cynthia Heimel observes:

> That giant thing they were striving for, that fame thing
> that was going to make everything OK, that was going
> to make their lives bearable, that was going to fill them

15. Just Jr., *Ongoing Feast*, 198: "It appears as if Luke has a double meaning here, one for the reader, who would connect redemption with the cross, another for the Emmaus disciples, who cannot see the cross as a means of redemption. Their concept of redemption was political, a freedom from Roman tyranny through a 'messianic' deliverer."

16. Keller, *Counterfeit Gods*, xiv.

with ha-ha-happiness *had happened*, and the next day
they woke up and they were still *them*. The disillusion-
ment turned them howling and insufferable.[17]

Jonah the runaway prophet said it best: *"Those who cling to
worthless idols forfeit the grace that could be theirs"* (2:8). The
walk on the Emmaus road reminds us that idolatry is the sure
way to despondency.

How Do the Disciples Finally Recognize Jesus?

In the beginning "their eyes were kept from recognizing him"
(24:16), but in the end "their eyes were opened, and they recognized him" (24:31). What causes the change? The answer might
disappoint. Jesus does not perform a miracle. A legion of angels
does not appear singing, "Glory to God in the highest." The
causes of change—again—are ordinary. Perhaps too ordinary.
Jesus has a Bible study with them and then a meal.

On the Emmaus road, Jesus basically opens the Bible and
says, "The entire Bible is about me." His message is clear: "If you
want to meet me, go to the Bible." But he doesn't simply say,
"Just read your Bible." Jesus specifies the way we should read
the Bible: "And beginning with Moses and all the Prophets, he
interpreted to them in all the Scriptures the things *concerning
himself*" (24:27). To encounter the risen Christ, we must read
the Bible intentionally, with the understanding that all of it
points to the person and work of Jesus Christ.[18]

The more common approach to the Bible is to read it with
the question, "What must *I* do to receive blessing in this life
and salvation in the life to come?" The protagonist of the gospel
story is no longer God but I. Read this way, the Bible becomes
a collection of stories from which we can draw inspiration and
guidance. When we obey what God commands, we feel great

17. Quoted in Keller, *Reason for God*, 167.

18. A brief but excellent recent treatment of this topic is Lillback (ed.), *Seeing Christ in All of Scripture*.

about ourselves and assured of God's favor. When we fail to do so, we become demoralized. This swing between self-righteousness and depression becomes exhausting. Eventually we either give up on trying to follow God or fall into the delusion that we're basically good people who occasionally lapse and that all God really cares about is that we try.

Jesus, however, offers a much better path. Our repeated failures should lead to neither depression nor delusion. Instead, they should remind us of two realities. On the one hand, we are so fallen that even with instruction and inspiration we fail to do what is right. Deep down every person knows this is true: the problem is not a lack of knowledge but a rebellious heart. On the other hand, our failures to be and do what God requires are meant to point us to Jesus Christ, the only One who ever loved God with all his heart, soul, mind, body, and strength. Reading the Bible with a "Christo-centric" hermeneutic is not just one approach among different options. It is the only interpretive approach prescribed by the Bible and consistent with our experience.

Indeed, adopting this approach to the entire Bible will yield much insight. Author Rebecca Jones says it this way:

> [W]e must also put each passage, each story, each proverb, and each commandment into the context of the grand story of history—that of Jesus Christ. We must ask of a passage, "What does this passage teach us about Jesus?" If we don't answer this question, we will never find the right moral application for our personal lives. Only as we see how a particular story increases our understanding of Jesus Christ will our vision be cleared to see what we should draw from that passage for our own use or for the use of the church.[19]

For instance, consider this famous story from the Old Testament. In Genesis 3, Adam and Eve eat the forbidden fruit. God then comes to speak with them. God wants Adam to take responsibility but Adam refuses to do so. Instead, he blames God

19. Jones, *Does Christianity Squash Women?*, 61.

("The woman whom *you* gave me . . .") and his wife (". . . *she* gave
me the fruit of the tree, and I ate") (Genesis 3:12). What moral
guidance or inspiration can we draw from this incident? That
men are cowardly? That good people keep rules? By contrast,
when we read Genesis 3 in light of Christ, we see that Jesus is
the Second Adam (Romans 5:12–20; 1 Corinthians 15:45–48).
Where the First Adam said, "Don't blame me—blame my wife
and punish her," the Second Adam says, "My wife is guilty, but
punish me in her place." By reading Genesis 3 in light of Christ,
we see that the passage points to Jesus Christ, the true husband.
He is the husband every woman wants and the husband every
man can become in him.

To be sure, the disciples do not yet perceive that the
stranger walking with them is the risen Lord Jesus. But in hind-
sight they perceive, "Did not our hearts burn within us while he
talked to us on the road, while he opened to us the Scriptures?"
(24:32). This "Christ-centered" Bible study was already working in them spiritual awakening. The fire from basic Bible study
was melting away their despondency and preparing them for
Jesus's full disclosure. We can be equally assured today that a
real and powerful encounter with the risen Lord can happen
through this sort of Bible study.

After the Bible study, the three sit together to share a meal.
It is at this point "their eyes were opened, and they recognized
him" (24:31). Some people explain the dinner scene this way:
when Jesus broke bread with the two disciples, it reminded
them of the last supper on the night before the crucifixion; this
recollection led to the revelation, "Behold, the Lord is with us."[20]
But this interpretation—while rich and intriguing—misses the
point. Wayne Beatty comments: "this was not the Sacrament.
This was an ordinary meal in an ordinary house, and it was
here, in the breaking of ordinary bread, that Jesus Christ made
Himself known to His followers."[21]

20. E.g., Lee, *Theology of the Open Table*, 160; Stein, *Luke*, 613.
21. Beatty, *Healing, Hope, and Joy*, 175.

Perhaps to the disappointment of some who feel the need to slay a dragon or bring back a witch's broom to meet the resurrected Lord, Luke says: "If you want to meet Jesus, spend time with Christians over simple meals." Through these ordinary means, you will meet the extraordinary Savior. New Testament scholar Hays writes: "In Luke 24, we have encountered the hint that resurrection-empowered reading occurs primarily in the context of a shared life in community, in the practice of breaking bread together."[22]

In her memoir *The Secret Thoughts of an Unlikely Convert*, Rosaria Champagne Butterfield recounts how the ordinary means of Bible study and meals changed her life. Once hostile to the faith, she recounts: "Stupid. Pointless. Menacing. That's what I thought of Christians and their god Jesus, who in paintings looked as powerful as a Breck Shampoo commercial model."[23] She then describes the impact of an unexpected friendship with a pastor and his wife:

> My Christian life unfolded as I was just living my life, my normal life. In the normal course of life questions emerged that exceeded my secular feminist worldview. Those questions sat quietly in the crevices of my mind until I met a most unlikely friend: a Christian pastor. Had a pastor named Ken Smith not shared the gospel with me for years and years, over and over again, not in some used-car-salesman way, those questions might still be lodged in the crevices of my mind and I might never have met the most unlikely of friends, Jesus Christ himself.[24]

22. Hays, "Reading Scripture," 236. Similarly, Shepherd Jr. comments: "[Bible] study alone is not enough. When the stranger attempts to go on ahead, the two disciples in the spirit of the ancient virtue of hospitality offer to share their bread and lodgings (24:29–30). This allows Luke to portray dramatically the experience of the risen Jesus in the Christian community, in such a way that no one could mistake how his disciples experience the continuing presence of Jesus" (*If a Sermon Falls in the Forest . . .*, 74).

23. Butterfield, "My Train Wreck Conversion."

24. Butterfield, *Secret Thoughts of an Unlikely Convert*, 1.

Butterfield relays how their ordinary friendship began:

> We had a nice chat on the phone, and Pastor Ken in-
> vited me to dinner at his house to explore some of these
> questions. . . Ken and Floy did something at the meal
> that has a long Christian history but has been function-
> ally lost in too many Christian homes. Ken and Floy
> invited the stranger in—not to scapegoat me, but to
> listen and to learn and to dialogue.[25]

Through these meals with Ken and his wife Floy, Butterfield
became more open to reading the Bible. She shares:

> I continued reading the Bible, all the while fighting the
> idea that it was inspired. But the Bible got to be bigger
> inside me than I. It overflowed into my world. I fought
> against it with all my might. . . Then, one ordinary day,
> I came to Jesus, openhanded and naked. In this war of
> worldviews, Ken was there. Floy was there. The church
> that had been praying for me for years was there. Jesus
> triumphed.[26]

Butterfield's conversion echoes what Luke teaches us in
this second resurrection appearance. Through the ordinary
means of Bible study and meals, people from all walks of life
can come to see the one resurrected Lord. This is God's kindness to those who are curious to know him. He doesn't ask for
the extraordinary. He simply invites them to study the Bible
and enjoy meals with his disciples.

In closing, we should observe how the two disciples change
upon recognizing the risen Son. Luke says that "they rose that
same hour and returned to Jerusalem" (24:33). They are filled
with astonishment and joy—so much so that irrespective of
danger and distance, they run back in the dead of night to tell
the others the good news. Chuck Clark describes it like this:

25. Ibid., 3, 11.
26. Butterfield, "My Train Wreck Conversion."

> After witnessing the presence of the resurrected Savior during dinner, those two disciples experienced a dramatic, personal change. They changed from Emmaus exhaustion to Jerusalem joy. Instead of staying in Emmaus . . . these two disciples were now traveling back to Jerusalem filled with excitement and hope! . . . They couldn't wait to get back to Jerusalem and tell everyone.[27]

An encounter with the risen Lord will bring about this sort of tangible change. Perhaps not right away, but eventually. Resurrection faith cannot help but change the disposition and direction of any person.

---

27. Clark, *Just Breathe*, 171.

5

The King Appears

Luke 24:36–53

IN LUKE'S FINAL RESURRECTION scene, an important shift takes place. New Testament scholar Darrell Bock puts it well: "Though Luke is concluding his Gospel, the real story is just beginning."[1] The conclusion of Jesus's earthly ministry initiates a new calling for his disciples. To this end, Jesus prepares them by confirming his bodily resurrection, orienting them to a new worldview, and summoning them to bask in prayer and worship.

Jesus Confirms His Resurrection

At dawn on the Sunday after Jesus died, several women went to visit his tomb and came running back with the shocking report that he had risen. Appalled by this brazen claim, the eleven disciples dismissed the women's account as a fairytale. Then two of them decided to leave. Jesus was dead, so there was nothing left for them in Jerusalem. But as they walked away, the risen Son pursued them. Later as they sat down to eat together, they realized it was Jesus himself. They then ran back to Jerusalem

---

1. Bock, *Luke 9:51–24:53*, 391.

to tell the eleven "what had happened on the road, and how he was known to them in the breaking of the bread" (24:35). Once again Jesus's disciples were confronted with the possibility of his resurrection. What a discussion (24:36) it must have been!

Now as they try to figure out what is going on, Jesus suddenly appears (24:36). This must have been shocking because the doors are locked. No wonder the first thing Jesus says is, "Peace to you!" (24:36). In contrast to Jesus's second resurrection appearance on the Emmaus road, the eleven disciples in Jerusalem immediately recognize him. But they remain confused. The last time they had seen Jesus, he was beaten, bloodied, and dead. So now the disciples "thought they saw a spirit" (24:37).

Noting their skepticism, Jesus asks, "Why are you troubled, and why do doubts arise in your hearts?" (24:38). Then, to dispel the notion that he is an apparition, he invites them to look closely at his wounds: "See my hands and my feet, that it is I myself" (24:39). The eleven collectively lean forward to peer at Jesus's outstretched hands and feet. Jesus then invites them not merely to look but also to feel his physical body: "'Touch me, and see. For a spirit does not have flesh and bones as you see that I have.' And when he had said this, he showed them his hands and his feet" (24:39–40). It seems to help, but "they still disbelieved" (24:41). To settle the matter, in consistent "resurrection fashion" Jesus does something ordinary. He asks, "Have you anything here to eat?" (24:41), and the disciples "gave him a piece of broiled fish" (24:42). A shaky hand extends the fish to Jesus, who "took it and ate before them" (24:43). As Jesus eats in their presence, the disciples stare at him in wonder, fixating on each detail as he takes the broiled fish, chews, and swallows.

There are two things we can take away from this encounter. First, as we have observed already, belief in the resurrection is difficult. If you are skeptical and wondering, "How could anyone believe in this sort of thing?"—that is exactly how the disciples felt. They were not naïve, nor were they predisposed to believe that people come back to life. After Jesus's crucifixion they were dejected, frightened, and filled with doubt even after several reports of Jesus's resurrection. For them, Jesus was dead. The end. So convinced were they of this that Jesus had to appear and give multiple evidences to prove that he was not a phantom. This encounter comforts us by presenting the founders of the church as extreme doubters of the resurrection. Indeed, ". . . the realistic response to all this involves a certain amount of skepticism."[2] Authors Jonathan Dodson and Brad Watson give this fitting encouragement:

> If you doubt the resurrection, I'm glad. Anything worth believing has to be worth questioning, but don't let your questions slip away unanswered. Don't reduce your doubts to a state of unsettled cynicism. Wrestle with your doubts. Find answers. . . Whether you are a skeptic, believer, or somewhere in between, press into your doubts and push back on your faith. Question your faith and question your doubts. Determine good reasons for believing or not believing in the resurrection of Jesus Christ.[3]

Jesus engaged the disciples on the level of his body because he wanted them to know that his resurrection was something they could verify in an empirical sense. Jesus wanted to make clear what the resurrection meant: an eating, living, functioning physical body. He was not a disembodied aura. Writer Stephen T. Davis comments, "[I]t does not follow from any of this that Jesus' raised body was not a material object;" rather, it was "something that took up space, occupied a certain location, *and could be seen*."[4]

Jesus also engaged the disciples in a physical manner to assure them that they were not hallucinating. He did this by appearing to them as a group. Psychologists Leonard Zusne and Warren H. Jones point out, "the fact that a phenomenon has

2. Shepherd Jr., *If a Sermon Falls in the Forest . . .*, 76.

3. Dodson and Watson, *Raised?*, 10–11.

4. Davis, "'Seeing' the Risen Jesus," 133.

been witnessed by many people does not exclude the possibility that it was a hallucination after all. There are collective hallucinations also."[5] But they highlight one critical factor:

> It is expectation that plays the coordinating role in collective hallucinations. Although the subject matter of individual hallucinations has virtually no limits, the topics of collective hallucinations are limited to certain categories. These categories are determined, first, by the kinds of ideas that a group of people may get excited about as a group, for emotional excitement is a prerequisite of collective hallucinations.[6]

As we have observed, the problem with a theory of "collective hallucination" to explain Jesus's resurrection is that the disciples were opposed to believing in his resurrection. They had no expectation or preparation. The opposite in fact is true. Author Gerald O'Collins comments:

> Theories of hallucination frequently suppose that after the death and burial of Jesus the disciples were eagerly expecting him to rise from the dead, and so deceived themselves into thinking that they saw him. The evidence from the New Testament suggests, however, that they did not persuade themselves, but needed to be persuaded when the risen Christ showed himself to them.[7]

The notion of a collective hallucination does not square with the fact that the disciples all dismissed what the women had said, that two of them left for Emmaus, and that the rest were hiding from Roman and Jewish authorities. All the criteria for collective hallucination are conspicuously absent.

Yet, in the end, the disciples came to believe in Jesus's resurrection through their collective encounter with him. Collectively they had all believed Jesus was dead and not coming back. And

5. Zusne and Jones, *Anomalistic Psychology*, 132.

6. Ibid. 135.

7. O'Collins, *Easter Faith*, 45.

collectively they could no longer hold to this belief. Faced with the evidence in front of them, the only rational response was to believe that Jesus had risen. Luke does not ask any of his readers to engage in "blind faith." Instead, he presses them to ask, "Given the disciples were not hallucinating and given they were predisposed not to believe in Jesus's resurrection, what changed them?" In other words, Luke challenges his readers to ask the hard but necessary question: how else can we explain the sudden change among the disciples apart from the resurrection?

Noteworthy and even inspiring is the experience of journalist Lee Strobel:

> As someone educated in journalism and law, I was trained to respond to the facts, wherever they lead. . . Yes, I had to take a step of faith, as we do in every decision we make in life. But here's the crucial distinction: I was no longer trying to swim upstream against the strong current of evidence; instead I was choosing to go in the same direction that the torrent of facts was flowing. That was reasonable, that was rational, that was logical. What's more, in an inner and inexplicable way, it was also what I sensed God's Spirit was nudging me to do.[8]

The second observation from Jesus's third resurrection appearance is the range of emotions the disciples exhibit. Look at the emotional roller coaster they experience: confusion and panic, uncertainty and marveling, joy and determination (24:37, 41). Luke relays this range of emotions because he wants to highlight the explosive and inevitable impact that the resurrection has. Jesus's resurrection confuses, unsettles, and even frightens; but ultimately it gives joy and peace. Jesus's resurrection is powerful enough to startle anyone out of complacency, depression, and purposelessness into focus, excitement, and purpose.

---

8. Strobel, *Case for Christ*, 267, 269.

Faith in the resurrection is not less than critical thinking. Jesus challenged his disciples to see, touch, and think. His resurrection was forcing them to reconsider what was possible. In *Where Good Ideas Come From*, Steven Johnson writes about invention and revolutionary breakthroughs. He observes that "error is not simply a phase you have to suffer through on the way to genius. Error often creates a path that leads you out of your comfortable assumptions. . . Being right keeps you in place. Being wrong forces you to explore."[9] So it is with our assumptions about the resurrection. At the same time, faith in the resurrection is not just critical thinking, that is, faith is not merely a cognitive exercise. Resurrection faith draws out an entire person and changes all of life. The resurrection is too radical to be left in the boring confines of trivial knowledge.

In Acts we see how the resurrection changes the lives of the disciples. These scared men are transformed into bold and compassionate champions of the gospel. They no longer fear death because Christ has overcome the grave. Gary R. Habermas and Michael R. Licona observe:

> After Jesus' death, the lives of the disciples were transformed to the point that they endured persecution and even martyrdom. Such strength of conviction indicates that they were not just claiming that Jesus rose from the dead and appeared to them in order to receive some personal benefit. They really believed it.[10]

Jesus Orients His Disciples to a Christian Worldview

Once Jesus convinces his disciples of his resurrection, he begins to revise their overall outlook. His resurrection demands that they adopt a new perspective on God, the Son, and the people of God.

9. Johnson, *Where Good Ideas Come From*, 137.

10. Habermas and Licona, *Case for the Resurrection of Jesus*, 56.

The first point Jesus highlights is God's sovereignty. Jesus reminds them that God is in control of every detail in history: "These are my words that I spoke to you while I was still with you, that everything written about me in the Law of Moses and the Prophets and the Psalms *must be fulfilled*" (24:44). The phrase "Law of Moses and the Prophets and the Psalms" refers to the entire Old Testament. In effect, Jesus was saying that God has been working in all of history to achieve his promised salvation: everything is working according to the purpose, promise, and power of God.

Yet, when we see war, disease, and natural disaster, we wonder. Frankly, it looks like God is doing a terrible job. Writer Jerry Bridges comments: "One of our problems with the sovereignty of God is that it frequently does not appear that God is in control."[11] The Bible addresses this apparent inconsistency by pointing to the cross. Jesus's emphasis on God's sovereignty is said in the context of his sufferings: "Thus it is written, that the Christ should suffer and on the third day rise from the dead" (24:46). Similarly, in his first public address, the apostle Peter declares, "this Jesus, delivered up according to the definite plan and foreknowledge of God, you crucified and killed by the hands of lawless men" (Acts 2:23). If we doubt that God is in full control, Jesus invites us to look at the cross and remember, "Even injustice and death could not thwart God's plans." Central to the new perspective Jesus instills is the understanding that suffering and sovereignty are not mutually exclusive.

Second, Jesus reiterates the centrality and necessity of his death and resurrection within God's plan of redemption. After he says that "everything written about me . . . must be fulfilled" (24:44), Jesus specifies *what* was written about him: "that the Christ should suffer and on the third day rise from the dead" (24:46). Jesus knew that many would think of him only as an inspiration or a hero who had died a premature death. Thus he reiterates the saving nature of his ministry: he died to pay the

---

11. Bridges, *Is God Really in Control?*, 33–34.

penalty of sin and was raised to life for our vindication. That is the gospel. This is the message of "first importance" (1 Corinthians 15:3).

That Jesus alone could die for the sins of humanity and that he alone was resurrected by the power of God means that he alone deserves our full allegiance and praise. The only human being that remotely mirrored Jesus in his compassion was Buddha. Buddha was a man born into comfort, wealth, and privilege. But when he saw the brokenness all around him, he decided to partake in the suffering of humanity by surrendering all his riches in hope that he might play some role in redeeming it. Yet, the important difference between Buddha and Jesus is that the former never claimed to be the Son of God. Indeed, he encouraged others to pursue and practice his teaching. But he never expected to be deified. Jesus, however, did not shy from receiving worship.[12] A truly consistent worldview does not posit Jesus as a friend or even counselor. He is the unique Lord and Savior who died and was raised to life to make in himself one new people.

The third part of Jesus's orientation is the all-inclusive scope of salvation. Jesus gives the disciples the instructions that "repentance for the forgiveness of sins should be proclaimed in his name to *all nations*, beginning from Jerusalem" (24:47). The qualifier is *all*—not some. Jesus wants his followers to bring

---

12. Vinoth Ramachandra writes: "When we explore the great religious traditions of the world, we come across many great figures who impressed their contemporaries with the other-centeredness of their way of life. They lived lives of exemplary courage, compassion and sacrifice. But such people make no grand claims for themselves, other than to be pointers to the truth. . . Gautama the Buddha 'saw himself as simply preaching the Dharma [truth].'. . . Likewise, in Islam, Muhammad is simply a prophet, albeit the final prophet, in a long tradition of prophets and messengers commissioned by God to turn people away from idols. . . But here Jesus stands out as different. You can search all the religious traditions of humankind—indeed I would go further and invite you to search all the great literature of humankind—and you will not come across one like Jesus, who makes seemingly the most arrogant claims concerning himself and lives in the most humble and selfless manner conceivable" (*Scandal of Jesus*, 18–19).

the gospel to every person in every place. Not only to people in third-world countries, but also to people in affluent suburbia. Not only to countries that are resistant to the gospel message, but also to countries where nominalism runs rampant.

There is indeed a certain irony to the Christian worldview. On the one hand, it is exclusive in the sense that it asserts salvation is found in Jesus alone. The apostle Paul puts it starkly in 1 Timothy 2:5–6: "For there is one God, and there is one mediator between God and men, the man Christ Jesus, who gave himself as a ransom for all, which is the testimony given at the proper time." All roads do not lead to heaven. On the other hand, the Christian faith is radically inclusive. Again, Paul writes: "it is pleasing in the sight of God our Savior, who desires all people to be saved and to come to the knowledge of the truth" (1 Timothy 2:3–4). Echoing the outward thrust of Jesus's own words, Paul highlights God's own desire to include people from all nations.

In this sense, a Christian worldview does not allow for racism, elitism, and discrimination. Discipleship requires repentance of such things and a commitment to share in Jesus's work of drawing people from every tribe, tongue, and nation into his "universal" family. Theologian Ronald J. Sider notes:

> In Luke's account of the Great Commission, Jesus commands his disciples to preach "repentance and forgiveness of sins" in his name (Luke 24:47). . . Biblical repentance includes turning from all sin including *social* sins. That means abandoning racist attitudes and neglect of the poor, indeed all that distorts human community.[13]

Acts details how this prepositional phrase "to all nations" changed the daily social relationships of the first Christians. In Luke's Gospel, all the disciples look the same. They're all Jewish, they're all from similar socio-economic backgrounds. They have one group of friends, one fraternity, one society. But in Acts, their friendships and community become radically

---

13. Sider, *Good News and Good Works*, 104–05.

diverse. Suddenly the first believers are developing deep relationships with people they would have never otherwise associated with. The gospel mandate to go "to all nations" had transformed them into a people of "all nations."

The purpose of this orientation is maturity. Kingsbury writes: "[Jesus] 'opens their minds' to comprehend the plan of salvation God accomplishes in him and thus leads them to spiritual maturity, and he commissions them to a worldwide ministry."[14] We tend to define spiritual maturity in terms of how pious a person's prayer sounds, how much theology and Bible he knows, or how diligently she serves. Jesus grounds Christian maturity in something less lofty but more powerful: being driven by the convictions that God is in control, Jesus uniquely saves, and the gospel is for everyone.

Jesus Encourages Prayer and Worship

In his conclusion, Luke highlights the need for continual and complete dependence on the Lord. The message is clear: for Jesus's disciples to serve as witnesses of the resurrection, they need divine power. This same point is made repeatedly throughout the Bible: salvation belongs to the Lord (Psalm 3:8). Indeed, when we remember this, we can share the gospel freely and confidently. Keller comments:

> Our dealings with others reflect humility because we know we are saved only by grace alone, not because of our superior insight or character. We are hopeful about everyone, even the "hard cases," because we were saved only because of grace, not because we were people likely to become Christians. We are courteous and careful with people. We don't have to push or coerce them, for it is only God's grace that opens hearts, not our eloquence or persistence or even their openness.[15]

14. Kingsbury, *Conflict in Luke*, 70.
15. Keller, *Center Church*, 49–50.

According to Luke, such dependence is expressed through prayer and worship.

After commissioning his disciples (24:48), Jesus instructs them to wait and pray for help: "And behold, I am sending the promise of my Father upon you. But stay in the city until you are clothed with power from on high" (24:49). Essentially, he tells them that they need the Spirit of Christ to continue the work of Christ. In this way Jesus guards his disciples from the idea that God had done his part and now it is up to them to do the rest.

The language of verse 49 is striking: "But stay in the city until you are *clothed with power* from on high." The work of sharing the gospel is a spiritual work. The apostle Paul makes this explicit elsewhere: "Finally, be strong in the Lord and in the strength of his might. Put on the whole armor of God, that you may be able to stand against the schemes of the devil. For we do not wrestle against flesh and blood, but against . . . the spiritual forces of evil in the heavenly places" (Ephesians 6:10–12). Given the autonomous streak in every human soul, it is easy to treat even the spiritual work of gospel-ministry purely as a human endeavor. We can begin to think that conversion is simply the product of human machination instead of divine intervention. The language of verse 49, however, reiterates that unless we are "clothed with power from on high," we tread into a spiritual battle naked and weak. For this reason, Jesus urges his disciples to wait and pray before anything else.

In addition to prayer, Jesus's disciples must engage in regular corporate worship. Luke makes this point by concluding his Gospel on a note of worship: "And they worshiped him and returned to Jerusalem with great joy, and were continually in the temple blessing God" (24:52–53). Apart from worship, our passion for missions dries up. Sunday worship is where we experience a renewed sense of God's love and power. God in his wisdom knows that we need to continue to receive grace in order to extend grace.

When we encounter the resurrected Christ, we feel the urge to connect with others who have experienced the same reality. This is why the first Christians continued to come together on Sundays. Not only were they compelled to go out *to* others to tell them about the resurrection; they were also compelled to come together *with* others because of it. I stress this point because today, especially in the West, the Bible's focus on worshiping together is often lost or ignored. As C. Franklin Brookhart points out, Christianity in America is commonly "private, soul focused, and emotionally validated. So pervasive are these that almost all of us assume them as part of our views of faith and belief."[16] The conclusion to Luke's Gospel challenges such assumptions. Brookhart observes:

> First, note that the account focuses on the gathered community, not on individuals. . . The gathered community is [the] locus of the narrative. Second, Jesus centers his attention on the community, and its ministry and identity. Indeed, the church is the focus of the rest of the New Testament.[17]

If you are exploring Christianity, Luke's concluding scene teaches that the best way to know Jesus and experience his resurrection is by joining a praying and worshiping community. You can read and study on your own—and you should. But in the end, Jesus is not an idea to be examined but a person to be encountered. God's normal design is for that encounter to take place through persons who have experienced the risen Son and now meet to celebrate grace. C. S. Lewis wrote that a person begins in

> a hall out of which doors open into several rooms. If I can bring anyone into that hall I shall have done my job. But it is in the rooms, not the hall, that there are fires and chairs and meals. The hall is a place to wait in,

16. Brookhart, *Living the Resurrection*, 89.
17. Ibid., 89–90.

a place from which try the various doors, not a place to live in.[18]

If we step back to consider this encouragement to pray and worship, we can appreciate something unique and extraordinary about Christianity. At the heart of the gospel is the declaration of the risen Son. He is not among the dead—he is risen. As the risen king, he desires a deep and personal relationship with his servants. Jesus is not an employer who has enlisted people to meet a quota of conversions. He is the loving king who has suffered with and for his people so that they would never feel alone. He does not want us to feel like his workers whose status depends on their performance. He does not want us to learn and share a set of impersonal facts. Instead, he desires us to have a continuous encounter with him because he has risen.

Serving as a witness to the resurrected Lord is not all that different from "witnessing" a good book, movie, restaurant, and vacation. Effective witnessing is most effective not when it is a rehearsed dissemination of facts but when it is an overflow of awe and enjoyment. A good movie, restaurant, or book does not require much official advertising. Its popularity will naturally spread from those who delight in it. This is the sort of witness Jesus wants. He wants his people to continually taste and know his goodness so that their witness can be a natural overflow of joy and awe. Thus, Jesus's encouragement to pray and worship is nothing other than a summons to continually encounter and enjoy the risen king.

18. Lewis, *Mere Christianity*, 10.

Bibliography

Bavinck, Herman. *Reformed Dogmatics, Volume 3: Sin and Salvation in Christ.* Edited by John Bolt. Translated by John Vriend. Grand Rapids, MI: BakerAcademic, 2006.

Beatty, Wayne. *Healing, Hope, and Joy: Faith-Based Reflections After a Traumatic Brain Injury.* Bloomington, IL: AuthorHouse, 2011.

Berger, Peter L. *The Sacred Canopy: Elements of A Sociological Theory of Religion.* New York: Anchor, 1967.

Billings, J. Todd. *Rejoicing in Lament: Wrestling with Incurable Cancer and Life in Christ.* Grand Rapids, MI: Brazos, 2015.

Bock, Darrell L. *Luke 9:51–24:53.* Baker Exegetical Commentary on the New Testament. Grand Rapids, MI: Baker, 1996.

———. *Luke: The NIV Application Commentary: From Biblical Text . . . To Contemporary Life.* NIV Application Commentary Series. Grand Rapids, MI: Zondervan, 1996.

Bridges, Jerry. *Is God Really in Control?: Trusting God in a World of Hurt.* Colorado Springs, CO: NavPress, 2006.

Brink, Laurie. *Soldiers in Luke-Acts: Engaging, Contradicting, and Transcending the Stereotypes.* Wissenschaftliche Untersuchungen zum Neuen Testament, 2 Reihe 362. Tübingen: Mohr Siebeck, 2014.

Brookhart, C. Franklin. *Living the Resurrection: Reflections after Easter.* New York: Morehouse, 2012.

Bruce, F. F. *Jesus: Lord & Savior.* Downers Grove, IL: InterVarsity Press, 1986.

———. *New Testament History.* New York: Doubleday, 1969.

Butterfield, Rosaria Champagne. "My Train Wreck Conversion." *Christianity Today.* February 7, 2013. http://www.christianitytoday.com/ct/2013/january-february/my-train-wreck-conversion.html. Accessed July 24, 2017.

———. *The Secret Thoughts of an Unlikely Convert: An English Professor's Journey into Christian Faith.* Pittsburgh, PA: Crown & Covenant, 2012.

Buttrick, David G. *The Mystery and the Passion: A Homiletic Reading of the Biblical Traditions.* Eugene, OR: Wipf and Stock, 2002.

Calvin, John. *Institutes of the Christian Religion Vol. 1.* Translated by Ford Lewis Battles. Edited by John T. McNeill. Library of Christian Classics 20. Louisville, KY: Westminster John Knox, 1960.

Carnahan, Joe, and Ian Mackenzie Jeffers. *The Grey.* Directed by Joe Carnahan. Open Road Films, 2011.

Carrier, Richard. "Why the Resurrection is Unbelievable." In *The Christian Delusion: Why Faith Fails,* edited by John W. Loftus, 291–315. Amherst, NY: Prometheus, 2010.

Carroll, John T. *Luke: A Commentary.* The New Testament Library. Louisville, KY: Westminster John Knox, 2012.

Carson, D. A. *Memoirs of an Ordinary Pastor: The Life and Reflections of Tom Carson.* Wheaton, IL: Crossway, 2008.

———. "Who is This 'Son of God'?" *Christianity.com.* http://www.christianity.com/god/jesus-christ/who-is-this-son-of-god.html. Accessed September 19, 2017.

Clark, Chuck. *Just Breathe: Learning to Inhale after Life Knocks the Wind Out of You.* Mustang, OK: Tate, 2013.

Conrad, Joseph. *Heart of Darkness and Other Tales.* Edited by Cedric Watts. New York: Oxford University Press, 2002.

Craig, William Lane. *On Guard: Defending Your Faith with Reason and Precision.* Colorado Springs, CO: David C. Cook, 2010.

Damon, Arwa, Ghazi Balkiz, and Brice Laine. "Why ISIS Offered to Kill this 4-Year-Old Girl." CNN. March 20, 2017. http://www.cnn.com/2017/03/30/middleeast/mosul-airstrikes-survivors. (Accessed April 1, 2017.

Davidson, Ivor J. *The Birth of the Church: From Jesus to Constantine, A. D. 30–312.* The Monarch History of the Church 1. Grand Rapids: Monarch, 2005.

Davis, Stephen T. "'Seeing' the Risen Christ." In *The Resurrection: An Interdisciplinary Symposium on the Resurrection of Jesus,* edited by Stephen T. Davis, Daniel Kendall, and Gerald O'Collins, 126–47. New York: Oxford University Press, 1997.

Dean, Robert J. *Leaps of Faith: Sermons from the Edge.* Eugene, OR: Resource, 2017.

Dicken, Frank. *Herod as a Composite Character in Luke-Acts.* Wissenschaftliche Untersuchungen zum Neuen Testament, 2 Reihe 375. Tübingen: Mohr Siebeck, 2014.

Dodson, Jonathan K., and Brad Watson. *Raised?: Finding Jesus by Doubting the Resurrection.* Grand Rapids: Zondervan, 2014.

Doran, Chris. *Hope in the Age of Climate Change: Creation Care This Side of the Resurrection.* Eugene, OR: Cascade, 2017.

Edgar, William. *Reasons of the Heart: Recovering Christian Persuasion.* Grand Rapids: Hourglass, 1996.

Edwards, James R. *The Gospel according to Luke.* The Pillar New Testament Commentary. Grand Rapids, MI: Eerdmans, 2015.

Engelmann, Kim V. *Soul-Shaping Small Groups: A Refreshing Approach for Exasperated Leaders.* Downers Grove, IL: InterVarsity, 2010.

Forbes, Greg W., and Scott D. Harrower. *Raised from Obscurity: A Narratival and Theological Study of the Characterization of Women in Luke-Acts.* Eugene, OR: Pickwick, 2015.

Frame, John M. *Systematic Theology: An Introduction to Christian Belief.* Phillipsburg, NJ: P&R, 2013.

Gillman, John. *Luke: Stories of Joy and Salvation.* New York: New City, 2002.

Gnuse, Robert Karl. *Trajectories of Justice: What the Bible Says about Slaves, Women, and Homosexuality.* Cambridge, UK: Lutterworth, 2015.

Gorman, Heather M. *Interweaving Innocence: A Rhetorical Analysis of Luke's Passion Narrative (Lk 22:66–23:49).* Cambridge, UK: James Clarke & Co, 2016.

Graham, Billy. *Just As I Am: The Autobiography of Billy Graham.* New York: HarperOne, 1997.

Habermas, Gary R., and Michael R. Licona. *The Case for the Resurrection of Jesus.* Grand Rapids, MI: Kregel, 2004.

Hanegraaff, Hank. *Resurrection: The Capstone in the Arch of Christianity.* Nashville, TN: Word Publishing, 2000.

Hays, Richard B. "Reading Scripture in Light of the Resurrection." In *The Art of Reading Scripture,* edited by Ellen F. Davis and Richard B. Hays, 216–38. Grand Rapids, MI: Eerdmans, 2003.

Hillenbrand, Laura. *Unbroken: A World War II Story of Survival, Resilience, and Redemption.* New York: Random House, 2014.

Hitchens, Christopher, and Douglas Wilson. *Is Christianity Good for the World? A Debate.* Moscow, ID: Canon, 2008.

Hugo, Victor. *Les Misérables.* Translated by Isabel F. Hapgood. New York: Thomas Y. Crowell & Co., 1887. https://www.gutenberg.org/files/135/135-h/135-h.htm#link2HCH0020. Accessed December 6, 2017.

Isaacson, Walter. "Steve Jobs, part 2." Interview by Steve Kroft. *60 Minutes.* CBS News. Aired October 23, 2011. https://www.youtube.com/watch?v=CXcfDN6L9d8&t=4s. Accessed August 2, 2017.

Jarvis, Cynthia A., and E. Elizabeth Johnson, eds. *Feasting on the Gospels: Luke, Volume 2: Chapters 12–24.* Feasting on the Word Commentary. Louisville, KY: Westminster John Knox, 2014.

Jensen, Morten Hørning. *Herod Antipas in Galilee: The Literary and Archaeological Sources on the Reign of Herod Antipas and its Socio-Economic Impact on Galilee.* Second edition. Wissenschaftliche Untersuchungen zum Neuen Testament, 2 Reihe 215. Tübingen: Mohr Siebeck, 2010.

Johnson, Steven. *Where Good Ideas Come From: The Natural History of Innovation.* New York: Riverhead, 2010.

Jones, Rebecca. *Does Christianity Squash Women?: A Christian Looks at Womanhood.* Nashville, TN: B&H, 2005.

Just Jr., Arthur A. *The Ongoing Feast: Table Fellowship and Eschatology at Emmaus.* Collegeville, MN: Liturgical, 1993.

Kadlecek, Jo. *A Desperate Faith: Lessons of Hope from the Resurrection.* Grand Rapids: Baker, 2010.

Keller, Timothy. *Center Church: Doing Balanced, Gospel-Centered Ministry in Your City.* Grand Rapids, MI: Zondervan, 2012.

———. *Counterfeit Gods: The Empty Promises of Money, Sex, and Power, and the Only Hope that Matters.* New York: Dutton, 2009.

———. *The Prodigal God: Recovering the Heart of the Christian Faith.* New York: Dutton, 2008.

———. *The Reason for God: Belief in an Age of Skepticism.* New York: Dutton, 2008.

———. "A Reason for Living." Sermon. February 27, 1994. http://www.gospelinlife.com/a-reason-for-living-an-open-forum-8066. Accessed June 17, 2017.

———. "With all this suffering, how could there be a God? Tim Keller at Veritas [7 of 11]." Interview by David Eisenbach. The Veritas Forum. Columbia University, February 2008. https://www.youtube.com/watch?v=dkn5lfutSrY. Accessed May 15, 2017.

Keyes, Dick. *Seeing Through Cynicism: A Reconsideration of the Power of Suspicion.* Downers Grove, IL: InterVarsity, 2006.

Kimbell, John. *The Atonement in Lukan Theology.* Newcastle upon Tyne, UK: Cambridge Scholars, 2014.

Kingsbury, Jack Dean. *Conflict in Luke: Jesus, Authorities, Disciples.* Minneapolis, MN: Fortress, 1991.

Lee, Eojin. *Theology of the Open Table.* Eugene, OR: Resource, 2016.

Lewis, C. S. *Mere Christianity.* In *The Complete C. S. Lewis Signature Classics.* New York: HarperOne, 2002.

———. *The Weight of Glory: and Other Addresses.* New York: HarperOne, 1976.

Lillback, Peter A. (ed.). *Seeing Christ in All of Scripture: Hermeneutics at Westminster Theological Seminary.* Philadelphia: Westminster Seminary Press, 2016.

Lloyd-Jones, Martyn. *Setting Our Affections Upon Glory: Nine Sermons on the Gospel and the Church.* Wheaton, IL: Crossway, 2013.

Loftus, John W. *Why I Became an Atheist: A Former Preacher Rejects Christianity.* New York: Prometheus, 2012.

Miller, Thomas A. *Did Jesus Really Rise from the Dead?: A Surgeon-Scientist Examines the Evidence.* Wheaton, IL: Crossway, 2013.

Mueller, Joan. *Is Forgiveness Possible?* Collegeville, MN: Liturgical, 1998.

O'Collins, Gerald. *Easter Faith: Believing in the Risen Jesus.* New York: Paulist, 2003.

Oliphint, K. Scott. *God With Us: Divine Condescension and the Attributes of God.* Wheaton, IL: Crossway, 2012.

Plantinga Jr., Cornelius. *Not the Way It's Supposed to Be: A Breviary of Sin.* Grand Rapids: Eerdmans, 1995.

Ramachandra, Vinoth. *The Scandal of Jesus.* Downers Grove, IL: InterVarsity, 2001.

Seo, Pyung Soo. *Luke's Jesus in the Roman Empire and the Emperor in the Gospel of Luke.* Eugene, OR: Pickwick, 2015.

Shepherd, Michael B. *The Twelve Prophets in the New Testament.* Studies in Biblical Literature 140. New York: Peter Lang, 2011.

Shepherd Jr., William H. *If a Sermon Falls in the Forest . . .: Preaching Resurrection Texts.* Lima, OH: CSS, 2002.

Sider, Ronald J. *Good News and Good Works: A Theology for the Whole Gospel.* Grand Rapids, MI: Baker, 1993.

Skinner, Matthew L. *The Trial Narratives: Conflict, Power, and Identity in the New Testament.* Louisville, KY: Westminster John Knox, 2010.

Stein, Robert H. *Luke: An Exegetical and Theological Exposition of Holy Scripture.* New American Commentary 24. Nashville, TN: B&H, 1992.

Stephenson, David. "The Gospel in Life, Part 4 (Luke 10:17–24)." Sermon. August 6, 2017. https://www.newcityva.org/resources. Accessed August 7, 2017.

Stevenson, Bryan. *Just Mercy: A Story of Injustice and Redemption.* New York: Spiegel & Grau, 2014.

Strobel, Lee. *The Case for Christ: A Journalist's Personal Investigation of the Evidence for Jesus.* Grand Rapids, MI: Zondervan, 1998.

Swoboda, A. J. *The Dusty Ones: Why Wandering Deepens Your Faith.* Grand Rapids: Baker, 2016.

———. *A Glorious Dark: Finding Hope in the Tension between Belief and Experience.* Grand Rapids: Baker, 2014.

Tannehill, Robert C. *The Narrative Unity of Luke-Acts: A Literary Interpretation, Volume 1: The Gospel according to Luke.* Philadelphia: Fortress, 1986.

Trueman, Carl R. "Messiahs Pointing to the Door." *Reformation 21.* March 2009. www.reformation21.org/counterpoints/wages-of-spin/messiahs-pointing-to-the-door.php. Accessed December 6, 2017.

Van Dixhoorn, Chad. *Confessing the Faith: A Reader's Guide to the Westminster Confessions of Faith.* Carlisle, PA: Banner of Truth Trust, 2014.

Vance, J. D. *Hillbilly Elegy: A Memoir of a Family and Culture in Crisis.* New York: HarperCollins, 2016.

Velotta, Jason R. *Reclaiming Victory: Living in the Gospel.* Mustang, OK: Tate, 2012.

Vitale, Vince. "A Response at the Cross." In *Why Suffering?: Finding Meaning and Comfort When Life Doesn't Make Sense,* edited by Ravi Zacharias and Vince Vitale, 81–104. New York: FaithWords, 2014

Volf, Miroslav. *Exclusion and Embrace: A Theological Exploration of Identity, Otherness, and Reconciliation.* Nashville, TN: Abingdon, 1996.

Wallace, J. Warner. *Cold-Case Christianity: A Homicide Detective Investigates the Claims of the Gospels.* Colorado Springs, CO: David C. Cook, 2013.

White, William L. *Recovery Monographs: Revolutionizing the Ways that Behavioral Health Leaders Think About People with Substance Use Disorders, Volume 1.* Bloomington, IN: AuthorHouse, 2015.

Woodward, James, Paula Gooder, and Mark Pryce. *Journeying with Luke: Reflections on the Gospel.* Louisville, KY: Westminster John Knox, 2015.

Wright, N. T. *Luke for Everyone.* London, UK: Society for Promoting Christian Knowledge (SPCK), 2001.

———. *The Resurrection of the Son of God.* Christian Origins and the Question of God 3. Minneapolis, MN: Fortress, 2003.

Yamazaki-Ransom, Kazuhiko. *The Roman Empire in Luke's Narrative.* Library of New Testament Studies. New York: T&T Clark, 2010.

Yancey, Philip. *The Jesus I Never Knew.* Grand Rapids, MI: Zondervan, 1995.

Zacharias, Ravi. "The Question." In *Why Suffering?: Finding Meaning and Comfort When Life Doesn't Make Sense,* edited by Ravi Zacharias and Vince Vitale, 1–30. New York: FaithWords, 2014.

Zusne, Leonard, and Warren H. Jones. *Anomalistic Psychology: A Study of Extraordinary Phenomena of Behavior and Experience.* Hillsdale, NJ: Lawrence Erlbaum, 1984.